A CREATIVE GUIDE TO

PATCHWORK & APPLIQUÉ

To Nikki and Philip

A CREATIVE GUIDE TO
PATCHWORK & APPLIQUÉ

LESLEY TURPIN-DELPORT

NEW HOLLAND

ACKNOWLEDGEMENTS

My special thanks go to Rachelle Druian, *to the artists from the Les Delport Studio*:
Caren Adno, Fiona Aronowitz, Orit Banai, Carol Been, Glenda Booth, Wendy Brodie,
Charles Broskey, Sharon Cane, Elaine Cohen, Jackie Crook, Anne Davis, Nikki Delport,
Linda Druker, Patsy Ellish, Briana Etzine, Adrienne Friedman, Gwen Gibbons,
Doreen Ginsberg, Simone Greenberg, Jill Hazelton, Wilma Hooper, Barbara Hughes,
Glynis Ismay, Michelle Jankelow, Ros Josset, Delyse Kramer, Joanne Lauter,
Julie Lazarus, Kim Lazarus, Diane Levine, Brenda Maraney, Elana Meyerson,
Sue Meyerson, Kathy Miller, Anne Neill, Cathy Newton, Terri Pryke, Ilana Radus,
Christopher Robin, Linda Ruskin, Lyn Sack, Maureen Sacks, Vivienne Samson-Sherwell,
Fay Scherer, Lesley Schnaid, Hazel Schwer, Jordy Seeton-Rogers, Blanche Sessel,
Rene Simon, Carol Slavin, Cal Smollan, Sheryl Stein, Anne Taitz, Megan Wallar,
Freydi Waner, Ilana Weiner and Pat Young *and to my photographers*:
Andy Arenstein, Tim Turpin, Ruedi Reimann and Rachelle Druian.

First published in the UK in 1988 by
New Holland (Publishers) Ltd
37 Connaught Street, London W2 2AZ
Reprinted in 1989, 1990, 1992, and 1994

ISBN 1 85368 003 6 (hbk)
ISBN 1 85368 120 2 (pbk)

Editor: Linda de Villiers
Designer: Jennie Hoare
Illustrator: Anne Westoby
Cover design: Abdul Amien
Phototypeset by McManus Bros (Pty) Ltd
Originated by Hirt & Carter
Printed and bound in Hong Kong by Dah Hua Printing Press Co., Ltd.

CONTENTS

INTRODUCTION

*T*here has been a wonderful revival of interest in crafts, particularly in appliqué, patchwork and quilting. These provide endless hours of pleasure and allow experimentation with design, colour and texture.

The origins of appliqué, patchwork and quilting date back to the late ninth century BC, and although all of them were used for hundreds of years in North Africa and the Middle and Far East, it was not until the late eleventh century that Europeans began to use appliqué and patchwork for decorative purposes. The Crusaders brought these techniques back to Europe after having seen the intricate banners and tents of the Saracens. The Europeans began to use these crafts for ornamental and utilitarian purposes – flags, banners, church vestments, wall hangings and quilts.

Quilting became very popular, especially corded quilting and trapunto, which was originally from Persia but perfected by the Italians. While these art forms waned in Europe during the nineteenth century, the North American settlers were patching and quilting with great enthusiasm. As times were extremely hard for the pioneers, these crafts thrived out of sheer necessity. Social gatherings were arranged for group quilting and gradually the simple, economic designs changed and specific designs, such as Log Cabin, Cathedral Window, Rose of Sharon and many more, developed. Now the American quilt, whether patchwork or appliqué, has become a traditional American folk art.

Today, with the exciting resurgence of the old crafts, new and special art forms are becoming evident. In compiling this book, I hope to illustrate the many sources of inspiration and the endless possibilities for interpretation of design and colour.

A project to design six pairs of slacks for Grace Jones was given to a young student from Leggat's School of Design. The delightful portfolio cover of Grace Jones in appliqué and the painting of two of the slacks show a splendid feel for design and a strong influence of appliqué concepts.

This appliquéd top was made by a young student from Leggat's School of Design. The open zigzag plays up the spiky feel of the black and cream hair. There is a fine balance of negative and positive shapes.

This appliqué was made from Andy Warhol's design of a wine label from the Mouton-Rothschild collection. The technique used is direct appliqué and one strand embroidery for the portrait details.

This textured and delicately conceived appliqué was created by Diane Levine from an illustration from the book **Where the Wild Things Are**. It was incorporated into the cover of this unique volume hand bound by her husband. Maurice Sendak kindly gave us permission to reproduce this delightful translation of his illustration. Notice the attention to detail.

This appliqué is a fabric collage. It was made as a gift for the student's husband who is an importer of haberdashery. Notice the attention to detail on the button cards.

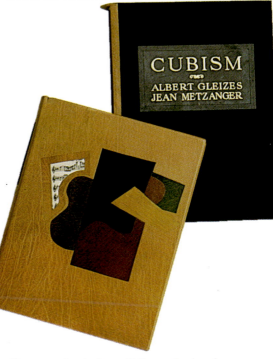

Two more books beautifully worked and bound by this husband and wife team.

This drawing was made by a student from Leggat's School of Design for an appliquéd jacket. An extremely sensitive drawing which could have many interpretations in appliqué, quilting and beads.

This intricate fellow was designed from the jesters on Scandinavian playing cards

PART ONE
BASIC TECHNIQUES

PATCHWORK

PATCHWORK is made by joining small patches of fabric together to make patterns. The *geometric design* which forms is the essential difference between appliqué and patchwork. The patches must be accurately cut and the fabric carefully planned. With clever placement of the patches and accurate joining, stunning results can be achieved.

There are so many traditional patchwork designs that I could not possibly go into this topic in depth, but the basic techniques described below will give the reader a guide to create and experiment and make new quilts which could be heirlooms of the future.

CHOOSING THE FABRIC

Fabric must be washable and colourfast. Choose finely woven fabrics, such as cotton, that fold easily. Avoid loosely woven fabrics which fray, such as stretch fabrics and synthetics. Sort the prints from the plain fabrics. Small prints are more suitable than larger ones. Fabrics should be of a similar type and all the same weight.

Leather is often used in patchwork garments because it does not fray. Velvet, linens and silks should only be used by advanced patchwork artists, as these fabrics are extremely difficult to handle.

Colours can be boldly contrasting or subtly shaded. Choose a basic pattern and work out the colour scheme. Begin by making a small piece of patchwork, such as a cushion, and master the basics before tackling patchwork that is more adventurous.

TEMPLATES

Templates must be made for each pattern piece in the block. Make these from cardboard, sandpaper or old x-ray plate. Sharp scissors, pencil, graph paper, set square, ruler, protractor and a pair of compasses are essential equipment.

Draw the template shape onto graph paper or simply trace a template directly from this book, and cut it out. Place the paper template on the cardboard, trace around it, and very accurately cut it out.

Three types of template can be used:

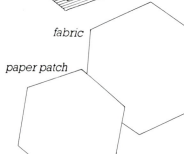

single template

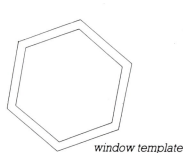

fabric

paper patch

two templates

window template

SINGLE TEMPLATE This is made the exact size of the finished patch. A 6 mm seam allowance is then added to the fabric.

TWO TEMPLATES One the size of the finished patch is used for the backing paper (page 11) and another with the seam allowance included, is used for the fabric patch.

WINDOW TEMPLATE This template is an empty frame; the inner edge is the size of the backing paper (finished patch size) and the outer edge is the size of the fabric patch with seam allowance included.

BASIC SHAPES

Most designs are based on the square which can be divided into triangles, rectangles and more squares. These basic shapes used in different proportions and combinations give rise to new geometric shapes, such as diamonds, parallelograms and trapeziums.

Other designs are based on the circle, or parts of the circle, to produce polygons such as hexagons, pentagons or octagons. Curved shapes are very difficult to piece together so they are usually hand-patched, or even appliquéd, to square patches which are then pieced together.

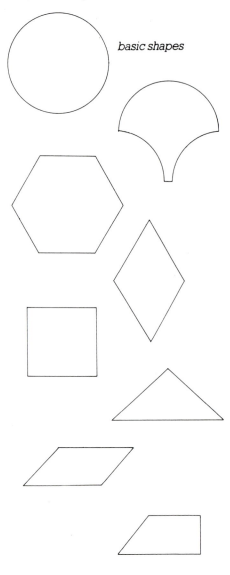

basic shapes

This is an exciting example of the potential in designing **patchwork from paintings** or **paintings from patchwork**. More examples of this principle appear at the end of this chapter. The original picture, drawn and coloured by a 12 year old art student, inspired the making of the patchwork. The basic shape is a trapezoid appliquéd onto the background. Imagine this delightful patchwork enlarged and made as a patchwork quilt with the ornaments appliquéd into the compartments!

PREPARING THE PATCHES

The purists believe the most accurate patchwork is achieved with paper backings (typing paper is ideal) and hand patching, especially for hexagons and curved shapes. A very fine, iron-on vilene interfacing can be used as a permanent backing but when quilted it does not produce the same rounded effect.

Cut the *paper backings* the exact size of the finished patch. Place the template on the paper, draw around the shape with a pencil and cut the paper as accurately as possible.

For the *fabric patches*, place the template on the wrong side of the fabric with one edge exactly on the grain line, parallel to the selvage. Draw around the template, remembering to add the 6 mm seam allowance unless it has been incorporated in the template already. Cut pieces patch by patch for accuracy and then sort out the patches according to colour and shape.

BACKING THE PATCHES The paper backing is attached to the fabric patch after both shapes have been cut out.

▶ Pin the paper patch to the wrong side of the fabric patch.

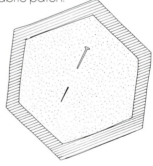

▶ Fold the fabric edges over and tack the fabric to the exact size of the paper. Press the folds into position with an iron.

▶ With triangular and diamond shapes, fold the edges to form sharp points.

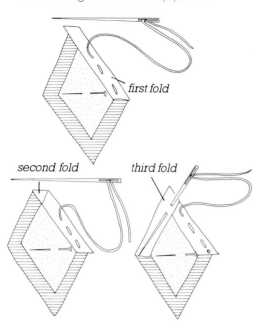

first fold

second fold   *third fold*

▶ Tack around the fabric edge of circles and curved shapes first. Place the paper patch in the centre of the fabric and pull the tacking thread gently until the circle fits the paper patch. Make a back stitch and cut off the thread.

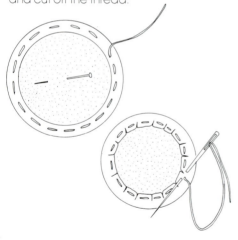

Now the patches can be pieced together to form blocks.

PIECING THE PATCHES

Piecing is the process of sewing all the small patchwork pieces together by hand or machine.

PIECING BY HAND The type of patchwork and the shapes used will determine which method of joining is best. The paper-backed fabric patches must be joined together with small, evenly spaced overcasting stitches. These stitches must be as invisible as possible. Join the patches in blocks, in rows or in one continuous piece.

Each block must make one complete pattern. Attach the blocks to each other in rows. When all the rows have been completed, whip stitch them together with right sides facing. Iron the completed work and remove the tacking and paper patches.

Patchwork shapes can also be pieced together without the use of backing papers. Place the fabric pieces right sides together and join them together with small, even running stitches, beginning and ending with a back stitch. Remember to maintain a perfect seam allowance of 6 mm. Press all the seams open or to one side.

Three examples of hand piecing are *Dresden plate* (page 56), *Baby Blocks* (page 49) and *Eight Point Star* (page 54).

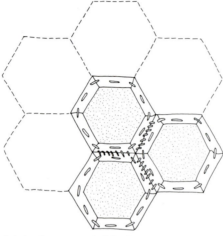

joining hexagons in blocks

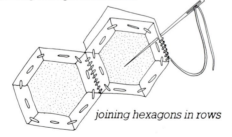

joining hexagons in rows

PIECING BY MACHINE Machine stitching is excellent for patchwork pieces with long, straight sides. Machine piecing is not recommended for curved patches.

Machine straight stitch the fabric patches, right sides together, maintaining a 6 mm seam allowance. Join the patches in rows and iron the seams open and flat or to one side. Join the rows together to form blocks.

One patchwork design that is ideal for machine piecing is Log Cabin. As it is slightly different from most other patchwork designs, I will describe the placement of the pieces in detail. The accompanying photographs illustrate two of the amazing results you can achieve by using the basic Log Cabin templates on pages 118-119.

LOG CABIN

This design is worked in square blocks composed of half light and half dark strips that are stitched and folded around a small centre square.
A foundation square of calico (the size of the finished block) gives strength to the patchwork and acts as a guide when positioning the strips.

▶ Fold and press two diagonal lines from corner to corner on the calico square to help you position the strips.

▶ Cut out the small centre square and pin it to the foundation (calico) square.

▶ Using templates 1 and 2, cut out pieces in light fabrics. Place strip 1 face down over the centre square. Machine straight stitch through all the layers 6 mm from the edge. Fold back the strip and press.

▶ Secure strip 2 in the same way.

▶ Cut strips in dark fabric using templates 3 and 4. Secure and fold these dark strips in the same way. The first circuit is now complete.

▶ Continue securing the strips in the same way, maintaining the light and dark patterning throughout.

When the required number of blocks has been made, join them in rows, right sides together, and stitch with a 6 mm seam allowance.

The light and dark halves of the block form different variations of the Log Cabin pattern, depending on how they are positioned: for example, medallions, open diamonds (see *Freydi's Log Cabin quilt* on page 58), diagonals, zigzags and windmills. Variations can also be achieved by attaching the strips in different ways, for example with the light and dark strips opposite each other instead of adjacent.

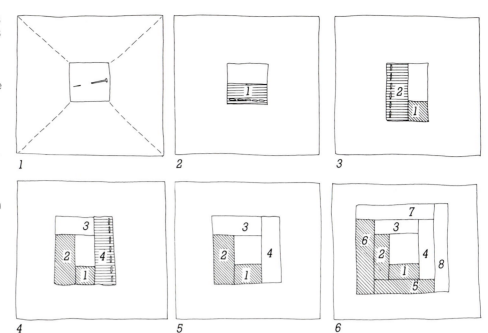

Above *This Log Cabin quilt illustrates the medallion design.*

Far left *Log Cabin patchwork can be machine quilted, if desired, by stitching along the seams of each strip to form radiating squares or by stitching on the diagonals.*

Left *This patchwork block best illustrates the arrangement of the light and dark strips in the Log Cabin design.*

FINISHING OFF

When all the blocks have been assembled, either by hand or machine, the patched fabric must be finished off. Fancy borders incorporating patterns from the main design can be used, or the fabric can be lined and edged with fabric bias binding (see page 42). Lining alone is only suitable for small patchwork pieces. Large patchwork pieces should be quilted to stabilize the fabric and for warmth. The different quilting techniques are discussed in full on pages 37-40.

The following measurements are the standard sizes for various quilts.

Cot	70 x 127 cm
Single bed	91 x 190 cm
Double bed	137 x 190 cm
Queen size	150 x 203 cm
King size	183 x 203 cm

Centre *This quilt has been finished off with a rolled, quilted border.*

Below *Notice the lace edging on the patchwork tablecloth in this appliquéd design.*

Right *Notice how the border echoes the central design.*

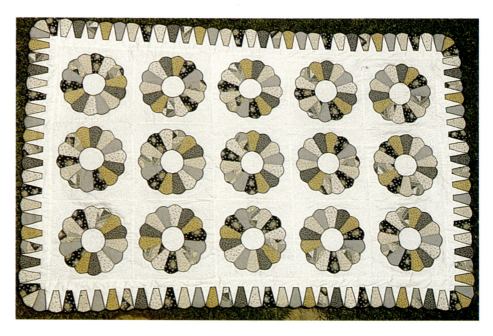

These drawings and paintings can be adapted and translated into magnificent patchwork.

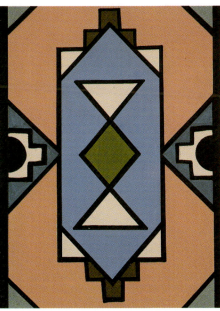

Top right The mesh work behind the soccer players inspired the painting of the quilt featured below.

Above This brilliant design of colour and concept created by one of my teenage art students would make an incredible patchwork quilt.

Left These Ndebele paintings show the basic geometric shapes that can be broken down into patchwork pieces and assembled to make stunning quilts.

APPLIQUÉ

APPLIQUÉ is the name given to the technique of applying one fabric to another. I have tried to keep the basic techniques as simple as possible but I have included some photographs to illustrate the complexity and intricacy which can be achieved if one understands the basic elements of this decorative craft.

How and where the appliqué will be used will determine the design and colour, which in turn will influence the choice of fabric, thread and stitching techniques. Although appliqué is essentially two-dimensional, the textures, stitches and shapes give it a third dimension.

Notice the excellent choice of fabric for the rabbit's face.

The balance of shapes, change in scale, and texture of fabric make this appliqué a work of art. The sense of distance is achieved through a reversal of light principles – the dark shapes are in the frontal zone and the yellow light in the distance picks up the ochre and yellow haystacks and ears of wheat.

SELECTING AND PREPARING FABRICS

Fabric choice will depend on the function of the appliqué. Is it functional or decorative? Will it be washed or have to stand up to wear and tear? Your choice will be further influenced if the appliqué is hand- rather than machine-sewn.

For hand appliqué, light or medium weight fabric is recommended. It should be easy to fold and closely woven. Natural fabrics such as lawn, chintz, gingham and light weight wools are best. This is only a guide as any fabric can be used if the appliqué artist is particularly talented.

Machine appliqué allows a far greater choice of fabric because the seam allowance does not have to be folded under as in hand appliqué.

Fine fabrics like silks, dacron, tulle and lace, as well as coarse, heavier fabrics, such as denim, corduroy, velvet, hessian, leather and suede, can be used. However, for garments and soft furnishings it is advisable to use fabrics of the same weight and durability. It is wise to pre-shrink the fabric and check that it is colourfast before use.

This delightful appliqué, inspired by a greetings card, has been entirely hand appliquéd. Full advantage has been taken of decorative and invisible stitches as well as gathered and stuffed shapes.

This detail shows an interesting combination of lace, chintz and satin. The fabric is machine satin stitched and the details embroidered by hand.

PLANNING THE DESIGN

COLOUR is personal but there are definite colour principles which you can use as a guide.

COMPLEMENTARY colours (opposite colours on the colour wheel) red/green, yellow/purple, orange/blue, create a visual vibrancy.

PRIMARY colours (blue, yellow and red) are dominant because they are pure colours.

JUXTAPOSED colours (those that lie next to each other on the colour wheel), such as blue, green and violet, blend together softly.

TONES are colours mixed with grey and are ideal for shadow areas because of their subdued nature.

TINTS are colours mixed with white and are excellent for highlighting.

NEUTRAL colours (black, white and grey) work well with any colour.

PATTERN AND TEXTURE The correct choice of pattern and texture is vital to the success of a design. Use geometric fabrics to create optical illusions, Granny prints for charm, and different textures for added dimensions.

This design is very subdued but the tactile quality of the different textures gives instant eye appeal.

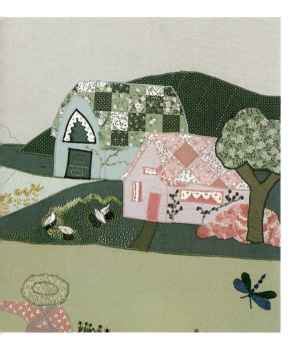

A good balance of patterned and plain fabrics has been used in this design.

ENLARGING THE DESIGN

Should you wish to enlarge your chosen design, trace it onto a sheet of tracing paper. Place the tracing paper over some graph paper so that you have a squared-up drawing.

If you find the squares on the graph paper too small, use a ruler and felt-tip pen to make an evenly squared grid on a larger scale, using the graph paper as a guide. Now draw another grid the size you would like the design to be. The second grid must have the same number of squares as the first.

Draw the design, square by square, referring to the corresponding squares on the original grid. It helps to number the squares on both grids.

original pattern

pattern enlarged on a grid

NOTE If the design is complicated, make a tracing from your enlarged design and use it as a top reference when assembling the fabric pieces on the background. Should the design consist of many pieces, it may help to number the pieces on the drawing.

TRANSFERRING THE DESIGN

IRON-ON VILENE is a transparent, bonded interfacing that is highly recommended for appliqué. Place the iron-on vilene, shiny-side up, over the design and trace onto the vilene with a pencil. Cut out the shapes and then iron them onto the fabric. The vilene strengthens the fabric and prevents unravelling.

TEMPLATES can be made if the design is simple or repetitive. Make the templates from cardboard or old x-ray plates.

DRESSMAKER'S CARBON AND TRACING WHEEL are also suitable. Place the carbon between the fabric and the design. Run the wheel along the design lines with enough pressure to transfer the lines onto the fabric.

A HOT TRANSFER PENCIL is excellent for marking designs on garments where the lines can be covered with fabric paint or beading.

A SECOND DRAWING can be made and cut up into pieces. Place the pattern pieces on the right side of the fabric, leaving 10 mm between the pieces to allow for seams. Draw around the pieces and cut them out, leaving a 5 mm seam allowance where necessary.

A DRESSMAKER'S PENCIL or a very light pencil can be used to draw designs directly onto sheer (transparent) fabrics.

HAND APPLIQUÉ

To transfer your design onto fabric, I find the iron-on vilene method the most successful. As there are different thicknesses of vilene available, choose the correct weight for your design. For example, if your design consists of a single layer of fabric, use a fairly thick vilene, but if it is made up of multiple layers, use a finer vilene.

▶ Place the vilene, *shiny-side up*, over the design. Trace each shape *separately*, using a soft pencil. Overlapping shapes must be drawn as though they were uninterrupted. It is not necessary to add seam allowances to the vilene.

design to be appliquéd

▶ Cut the vilene pieces and place them, shiny-side down, onto the wrong side of the fabric, leaving at least 10 mm between each shape for the fabric seam allowance.

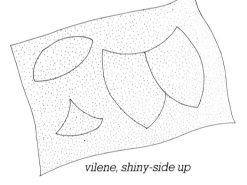

vilene, shiny-side up

▶ Iron on the vilene and cut out the fabric shapes leaving a 5 mm seam allowance of fabric around each vilene shape.

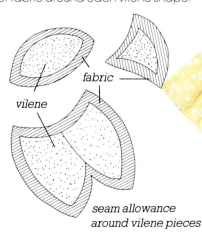

vilene

fabric

seam allowance around vilene pieces

▶ Begin the hand appliqué by turning under the seam allowances. Fold the fabric at the edge of the vilene and tack along the fold around each piece.

▶ *Curved* edges must be clipped and notched to make a perfect shape.

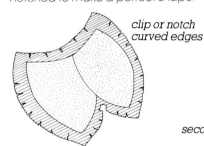

clip or notch curved edges

▶ *Corners* can be turned and folded (like a parcel) or mitred to give good points.

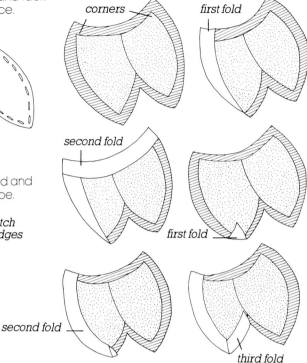

corners   *first fold*

second fold

first fold

second fold

third fold

These little figures are very difficult to create. The fabric is cut slightly larger than the original drawing, partly hemmed in place and stuffed as the shape grows. Once the shapes are attached, the face details are made by soft sculpting using matching thread.

19

▶ Once the seam allowances have been turned under and tacked, attach the shapes to the background fabric.

▶ *Single shapes* can be attached by using any of the variety of stitches described on page 20.

▶ *Multiple shapes* can be whip stitched (page 20) together first (see Patchwork page 12) and then attached to the background. An alternative method of assembling multiple shapes is to lap the top shape over the lower shape's raw edge.

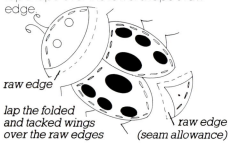

raw edge

lap the folded
and tacked wings
over the raw edges   *raw edge*
                                 (seam allowance)

▶ Another method of assembling hand appliqués is to fold the seam allowances under, pin the shape directly onto the background and stitch the shape in place. This method is ideal if the shapes are going to be stuffed. A few appliqué stitches are made, the stuffing is tucked into place and the stitching is then completed.

HAND APPLIQUÉ STITCHES Tiny whip stitches, running stitches, blind hem-stitches and back stitch, as well as a variety of decorative embroidery stitches, are all suitable for securing hand appliquéd designs to the background fabric.

Back stitch and whip stitch give a flat edge and are very secure. Blind hem-stitch gives a soft, rounded edge.

BLIND HEM-STITCH These stitches should be almost invisible. Bring the needle through the fold of the seam allowance and pick up a few threads of background fabric. Re-insert the needle through the fold and slide it along the fold for about 5 mm. Bring the needle through the fold and pick up a few threads of background fabric. Continue in this way around the appliqué shape.

RUNNING STITCH Weave the needle in and out of the fabric just inside the folded edge of the appliqué, taking tiny stitches through both the appliqué and background fabric.

WHIP STITCH Bring the needle up through the appliqué a small distance from the edge and re-insert it into the background at the edge of the appliqué, making a small diagonal stitch. Continue stitching, maintaining the diagonal.

This is a beautiful example of hand appliqué. The sensitive handling of difficult fabric and a perfect choice of blind hem-stitch shows clearly in this piece of work.

BACK STITCH This stitch resembles machine straight stitch. Make a small stitch just inside the folded edge of the appliqué. Leave a small space and come up the same distance away as the length of the first stitch. Insert the needle at the end of the first stitch, thus making a small back stitch.

blind hem-stitch

running stitch

whip stitch

back stitch

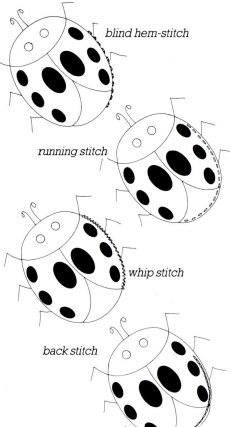

This appliqué is very advanced. Gathered and stuffed shapes have been used for added dimension.

Shapes can also be *hand embroidered* to the background using a selection of embroidery stitches. This method is both decorative and functional (see pages 28 and 29). Embroidery defines the outlines of the shapes and is a particularly good method for attaching stuffed or quilted shapes to the background fabric.

SHADOW APPLIQUÉ is another hand appliqué technique using transparent fabric to create a very subtle and delicate effect which gives a gentle diffusion to the basic appliqué shapes.

▶ Transfer the design onto vilene, cut out the shapes and iron them onto your choice of fabric. Cut out the fabric shapes without adding fabric turn-under seam allowances.

▶ Assemble the design directly onto the background fabric using a commercial glue stick.

▶ Cut a piece of *sheer* fabric the same size as the background fabric. Position it over the appliqué prepared background and tack the layers together on the diagonal.

▶ Using sheen or embroidery thread slightly darker than the sheer fabric, make tiny running stitches through all the layers, just inside the edges of all the appliqué pieces. Add embroidery details, if desired, at this point.

If a quilted effect is required

▶ Cut pieces of batting and lining the same size as the background fabric and sandwich the batting between the wrong side of the lining and the completed top. Tack the layers together.

▶ Quilt around each appliqué shape using tiny running stitches. The design will have a shadowy effect with a double line of running stitches around each shape.

▶ To complete the design, quilt the background with French knots (page 28) or echo quilting (page 39), if desired.

If a quilted effect is not required

▶ Omit the batting and lining instructions and make the second row of running stitches, just outside the fabric shapes. The double row of running stitches must encase the fabric design. (This type of shadow appliqué is ideal for tablecloths or if both the background and top fabric are sheer.)

MACHINE APPLIQUÉ

Machine appliqué is stronger and faster than hand appliqué. The raw edges are covered with a closed zigzag stitch. A close, narrow zigzag setting will give a definite, ridged satin stitch while a slightly open setting will give a more zigzag-like pattern. A fairly narrow width (approximately 2 on most machines) and quite close zigzag (approximately ½) is suitable for most work. Bobbin tension can be a little tighter than usual as this will pull the top threads through to give a well-rounded top satin stitch. Good thread must be used for a satiny finish.

The colour choice of thread will depend on whether the design requires delineation with a contrast thread or, if the colour zones are sufficiently marked, with a matching thread.

Notice the subtle choice of fabric colours and embroidery details in this shadow appliqué.

DIRECT APPLIQUÉ Prepare the shapes by using the iron-on vilene technique as follows:

▶ Place the vilene, *shiny-side up*, over the design and trace each shape separately using a soft pencil. Draw all the details onto each piece.

▶ Where two raw edges will meet, an *underlap seam allowance* of 5 mm must be marked on one piece on the vilene. This seam allowance will be tucked under the adjacent piece when assembled. The underlap allowance is only added to the piece that will not change the design when the pieces are assembled. *Superimposed* pieces do not require underlap allowances.

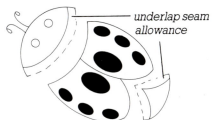
underlap seam allowance

▶ Cut out the shapes on the marked outlines and then iron the vilene shapes, shiny-side down, onto the wrong side of the fabric. Remember that the straight grain of the appliqué shape must run in the same direction as the straight grain of the background fabric so as to prevent puckering and stretching.

▶ Cut out the fabric shapes following the vilene outlines. The vilene-backed shapes are now ready to assemble.

▶ Place the shape *directly* onto the background and tack in place. Tack close to the edge in matching thread so that the zigzag stitches will cover the tacking. A glue stick can be used to secure small pieces before machining.

▶ Set the machine on straight stitch, with width on (0) and length on (0) to knot the threads underneath. End your work in the same manner when changing thread or completing a shape. Now machine satin stitch, working from the centre outwards. Be sure the needle is very sharp and check that the needle enters the fabric from the raw edge, inwards.

▶ At a corner leave the needle in the fabric on the outside of the line of stitches, lift the foot, then turn the fabric and continue stitching so that the first stitch overlaps the previous stitch.

▶ The direct appliqué method is suitable for designs that are not too large or complex.

DOUBLE VILENE TECHNIQUE This is a technique suitable for designs that are too large to pass comfortably through a machine, for example quilts, shapes that are going to be heavily embroidered or beaded and for designs on garments (for example T-shirts and jackets). Shapes are machine stitched first and then attached to the background fabric by hand or machine. A slightly raised effect is also an interesting aspect of this technique.

▶ With the vilene *shiny-side up*, trace the shapes in the design onto the vilene using a soft pencil. Add an underlap seam allowance where two raw edges will meet. Superimposed pieces do not require an underlap allowance.

▶ Cut out the vilene shapes on your marked outlines.

▶ Iron the vilene shapes, shiny-side down, onto the wrong side of the appliqué fabric.

▶ Cut out the fabric shapes following the vilene outlines. Now the *second* piece of vilene is used – hence the name 'double vilene technique'.

▶ Assemble the shapes according to your design onto another piece of iron-on or ordinary vilene. The vilene must be large enough to protrude all round the edges of the design. Superimpose and underlap where necessary. Tack or glue the pieces in position. If iron-on vilene is

used, tack or glue the pieces onto the *dull* side.

▶ Place the design in the machine and satin stitch all the raw edges.

▶ Carefully cut away the excess vilene without cutting into the zigzag stitching. If necessary embellish the design as required with embroidery, beading or decorative stitching.

▶ Place the design onto the background fabric and secure it by hand, using a small blind hem-stitch (page 20) over the satin-stitched edge; or by machine with an open zigzag over the satin-stitched edge, in the same colour thread. A straight stitch just inside the overlocked edge is also suitable. If iron-on vilene is used, the design can be ironed, instead of tacked, onto the background, provided the design is not beaded or heavily embroidered.

DOUBLE FABRIC TECHNIQUE This is an extension of the double vilene technique. This technique is used when 3-D shapes or reversible free-form images are required. Instead of using a second piece of vilene as backing, place the shapes on another piece of fabric. Satin stitch the shapes and cut away the excess fabric. These shapes can be stuffed very successfully.

The double vilened birds are tacked onto the background with the transparent fabric placed over the webbed feet to give the illusion of water.

Notice the contrast fabric on the underside of the wing.

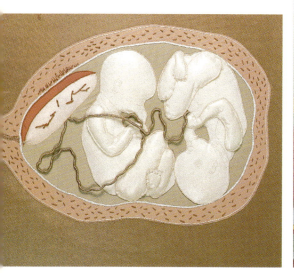

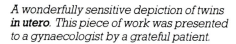

A wonderfully sensitive depiction of twins *in utero*. This piece of work was presented to a gynaecologist by a grateful patient.

These houses form part of a large wall hanging. Each house is double vilened, embroidered and then assembled onto another block. These blocks are then joined together to make up the complete wall hanging.

This series of moths shows the ideal use of the double vilene technique. Each moth has been overlocked, heavily embroidered and hand-hemmed onto the sheer, silk organza background. This piece of work was created by the author and her 12 year old daughter and took nine months to complete.

PART TWO
ADDED DIMENSIONS

PROBABLY the most exciting aspect of this absorbing craft is the addition of embroidery, woollen loops (for hair), beadwork, fancy machine stitches, quilting and free-form shapes. These are the finishing touches that can transform a piece of appliqué or patchwork from the ordinary to a work of art.

EMBROIDERY

Embroidery is like painting with a needle and thread. The stitches described below are ones I find particularly useful for appliqué design details.

BASIC EQUIPMENT Before you begin, make sure that you have the following basic equipment.

NEEDLES A good selection of very sharp to blunt-tipped needles (for wool or weaving) is essential.

SCISSORS Small sharp-pointed.

THIMBLE (for leather work).

THREAD It is handy to have different types of embroidery thread. There is an excellent selection available: Six-strand cotton, pearl cotton, crewel wool, metallic thread, crochet cotton and new textured wools, to mention just a few.

BEES WAX to prevent knots and tangles.

EMBROIDERY RING to keep the ground fabric taut while the embroidery is being worked.

FABRICS Any fabric is suitable for decorative embroidery. The appliqué or patchwork background will dictate your choice of threads and stitch techniques.

This work is still in progress and is a combination of hand-appliquéd laces and cords, machine twin-needle stitching and hand embroidery. It is a neutral interpretation of Melrose House, an historical monument in Pretoria:

Iron-on vilene has been used here to transfer the embroidery design onto the background fabric. (Work in progress)

TRANSFERRING THE DESIGN There are a number of methods of transferring designs onto fabric.

IRON-ON VILENE is invaluable for the crafts person who cannot draw well. Place the vilene, *shiny-side down,* onto the design. Trace the design onto the vilene, cut out the shape and iron it directly onto the appliqué or patchwork. By the time the design is complete, the vilene will not be noticeable.

TRACING PAPER TRANSFER Use masking tape to attach your design to a window pane. Place a piece of tracing paper over it and trace the outlines with a pencil. Go over the design on the reverse side of the tracing paper, place this against your fabric and draw over it with enough pressure to transfer the design.

HOT-TRANSFER PENCIL Trace your design onto tracing paper and go over the back of the design with a hot-transfer pencil. Iron the design onto the background fabric.

EMBROIDERY, BEADWORK AND QUILTING

buttonhole stitch

couching (or laid work)

Pekinese stitch

bullion rosebud

bullion knot

French knot

satin stitch

grub rose

split stitch

fly stitch

extended French knot

spider's web

Roumanian stitch

detached chain stitch (lazy daisy)

stem stitch

chain stitch

back stitch

raised chain stitch

long & short satin stitch

TRACING DIRECTLY FROM DRAWING
This can only be done if the fabric is
transparent. Place the fabric over the
design and trace over the outlines with a
pencil. Use dressmaker's pencils in pink,
blue or white or a fabric pen which
washes out or fades after 24 hours.

DRESSMAKER'S CARBON Trace the
design onto tracing paper. Place the
dressmaker's carbon face down
between the ground fabric and the
tracing. Go over the outlines to transfer
the design.

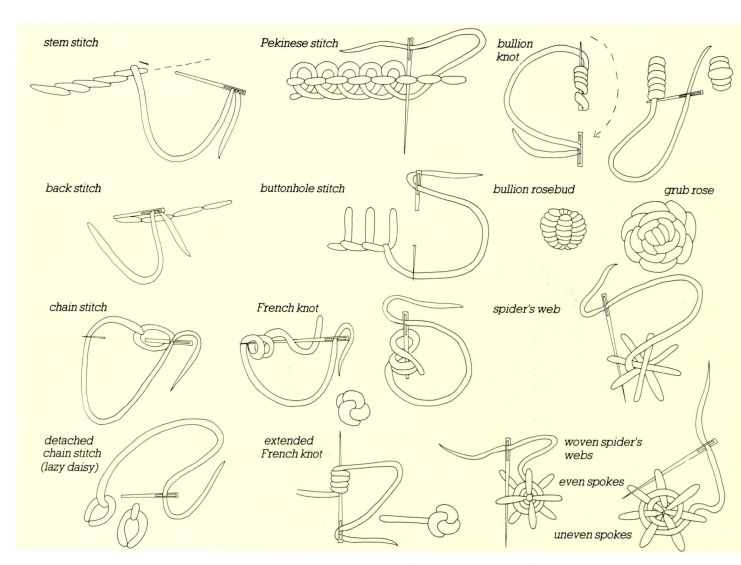

stem stitch

Pekinese stitch

bullion knot

back stitch

buttonhole stitch

bullion rosebud

grub rose

chain stitch

French knot

spider's web

detached chain stitch (lazy daisy)

extended French knot

woven spider's webs

even spokes

uneven spokes

HAND EMBROIDERY Most fine embroidery is worked using two strands of six-strand embroidery thread. Bullion knots and French knots work well with three strands, while grub roses require all six strands. For bold effects, use many strands of embroidery thread or wool yarn but do use thread that is compatible with your ground fabric, that is silk on silk, cotton on cotton and so on.

Cut your threads about 20 cm long and wax them, if necessary, to prevent tangles and knots. Begin and end with a back stitch and not a knot.

Notice the use of long and short satin stitch, spider's web and fly stitch.

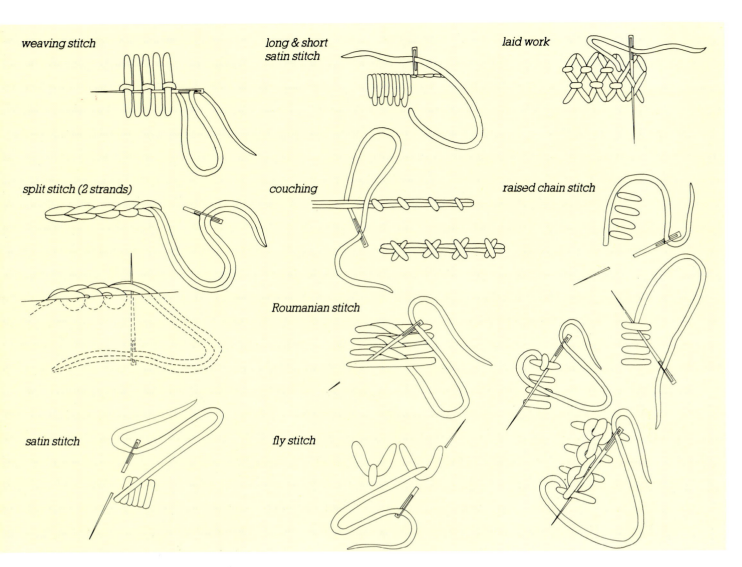

weaving stitch

long & short
satin stitch

laid work

split stitch (2 strands)

couching

raised chain stitch

Roumanian stitch

satin stitch

fly stitch

Bullions and extended French knots have
been used to create the flowers.

These embroidered fantasy birds make full use of all the embroidery stitches previously described.

These grub roses were made using six-strand, 11 twist bullions. The first three parallel bullions are in the darkest shade; then the next four bullions are in a paler shade making a circular shape around the centre and slightly lapping each other. The palest shade is used for five and then seven bullions, following the same circular rhythm.

It is attention to detail, like these embroidered flowers using split stitch, extended French knots, buttonhole and bullions, that accounts for the success of an appliqué picture.

These photographs show more interesting embroidery combinations for creating flowers on appliqué backgrounds.

The embroidery details on these moths are an artist's interpretation in thread of the actual markings on the real moths.

WORKING WITH WOOL

All the embroidery stitches illustrated on pages 28 and 29 can also be worked in wool to create exciting added dimensions to your work.

Traditional embroidery stitches, combined with a creative imagination, result in this type of work. When using 'chunky' wools, it is best to use couching or any of the woven stitches.

Embroidery worked on this scale is quick and easy and the effect dynamic.

Woollen fabric also gives texture and dimension.

This design uses interesting wools, metallic threads and traditional embroidery stitches.

The charm of this appliqué lies in the clever choice of different woollen fabrics for the animals. The texture of the fabrics gives the design a tactile quality.

WOOLLEN LOOPS can be used to create hair. One method is to bend a *wire hanger* into a U-shape and then wind the wool around the wire as shown. Machine straight stitch along the middle of the wool, sliding the woollen loops off the hanger as you proceed. These loops can then be stitched onto the appliqué.

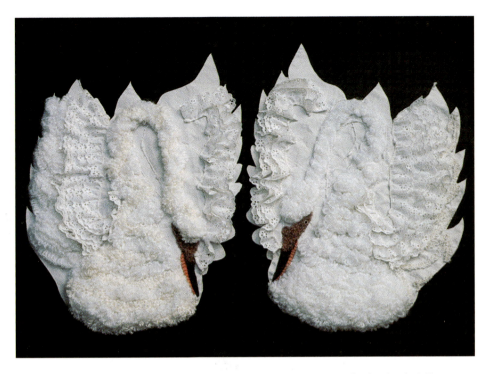

u-shaped wire hanger

woollen loops

Another method of making loops is with a metal *looping foot*. Set the machine as for appliqué satin stitch (zigzag with a stitch width of about 2 and a stitch length of about ½). When turning corners, lift the needle out of the fabric, raise the presser bar and push the loops off the metal shaft. Swivel the fabric, lower the presser bar and continue looping. The looping must be manually knotted off on completion.

These swans are made up of woollen loops and anglaise lace attached to basic fully-overlocked swan shapes.

This humorous design is heightened by attention to details like the doctor's woollen loop hair and moustache and the nurse's ginger looping foot hair.

The woollen abdomens of these moths were made by cutting and trimming the woollen loops once they were securely attached to the suede background.

Silk hair can be created by pulling off coils of *gown cord* to make ideal ringlets. Attach the coils by couching them onto the appliqué.

Another use for cord is the effect achieved by making a front door by couching soutache (cord), and then knotting and turning it as it is attached. This technique is excellent for tree trunks and bird's nests as well (see the nest on page 66).

Soutache has been couched and knotted to create this door.

Notice all the different hair techniques.

This little girl has silk hair made from an unravelled gown cord.

PETALS AND FLOWERS

SILK FLOWERS These little flowers are purchased from decorating shops and have plastic stems. Pull the silk petals from the plastic stem and reassemble the blooms onto the appliqué, connecting the petals with attractive embroidery stitches such as French knots, bullions and spider's web (page 28).

These petals have been attached with bullion knots.

34

Larger silk flowers can be attached with beads and used to decorate T-shirts and tops.

FREE-FORM PETALS

FREE-FORM PETALS are made by stitching two shapes together, turning through and attaching to the appliqué.

With right sides together, machine straight stitch the shapes together, leaving a small opening for turning through. Trim the seam allowance, clip any curves and turn through. Now lightly stuff the shapes. Top quilting can be added to give the petals definition.

Attach the petals to the background and satin stitch in place, closing the opening at the same time.

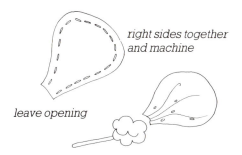

right sides together and machine

leave opening

clip curves, turn through and stuff

THREE-DIMENSIONAL PETALS

THREE-DIMENSIONAL PETALS These petals are made from suede or soft leather and are attached to garments.

Using the pattern on page 173, cut out five petals and a circle for the centre of the flower. Take a double thread and string the five petals onto it. Pull up the thread tightly, gathering the petals to form a circle. End off with a strong back stitch.

Run a gathering thread around the edge of the suede or leather circle and pull up, inserting a piece of batting as you tighten the circle so that it resembles a stuffed button. Attach the ring of petals to the back of the stuffed centre with whip stitches. Decorate the centre with beads, if desired.

A small piece of Velcro can be stitched to the back of the flower and to the garment so that the flower can be removed before washing.

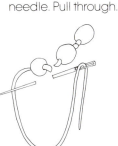

BEADS AND SEQUINS

Beads and sequins can add glamour and dazzle to appliquéd garments or, for a more subtle effect, use beads in combination with appliqué. (See eyes of the Goosander chicks on page 66.)

The selection of beads available is fantastic, ranging from tiny glass beads, rhinestones and clay beads to carved, wooden beads. For appliqué, I would recommend the following three basic types:

▶ Tiny glass beads in a variety of colours both opaque and transparent

▶ Bugle beads in various lengths and colours

▶ Sequins in different shapes and sizes

BEADS should be placed neatly together in a pre-arranged order. A very long, thin needle with a tiny eye is a must. Choose the thread colour to suit your article and use a double thread, beginning and ending with a knot and a back stitch for extra strength.

INDIVIDUAL BEADS To attach individual beads, bring the needle through the fabric, thread the bead onto it and pull through. Insert the needle next to the first exit and make a stitch slightly longer than the bead with the thread below the needle. Pull through.

The bead details were worked to give added interest to the centre of this double vilene appliqué design. On completion, the beaded appliqué was then hand-hemmed onto the ground fabric.

Rose featuring free-form petals.

Notice the use of basic techniques and clever adaptations.

Individual, large beads can also be attached with a tiny seed bead.

As there are several quilting techniques to choose from, it is important to select one that will enhance the appliqué or patchwork. The following are some of the quilting methods available.

DIAGONAL QUILTING Stitch diagonal lines at regular intervals across the top of the quilt in one direction and then at the same intervals in the opposite direction to form a diamond pattern.

This cushion has been diagonal quilted by hand.

This quilt has been diagonal quilted by machine – notice the diamond pattern.

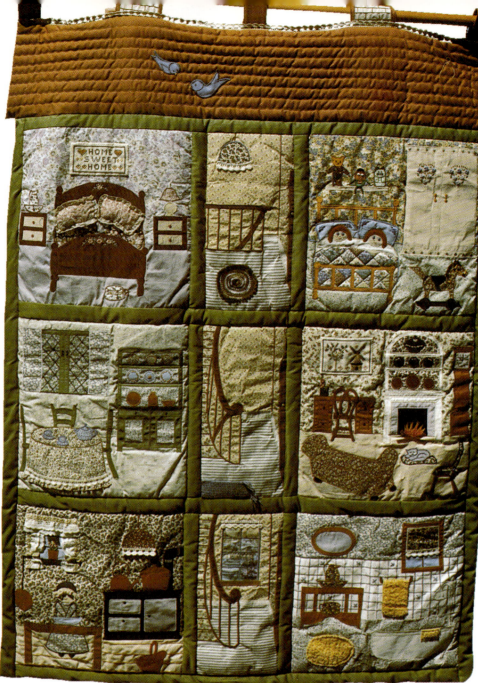

Each room of the doll's house was appliquéd and quilted, joined two rooms at a time and then row by row until the wall hanging was complete.

TIED AND BUTTONED QUILTING Another method of sewing the patchwork, batting and lining together is called tied quilting. This method is best if wool batting is used in place of polyester, as it is generally too thick for conventional quilting. The three layers are knotted together at regular intervals but although quicker, this method is not as decorative as stitched quilting.

Use an embroidery needle and wool or embroidery thread and make one stitch through all the layers, leaving a long end on top of the quilt. Make a back stitch and bring the needle up to the top again. Tie the ends together into a strong knot or tight bow.

Buttons can also be used to create a quilted effect. Secure a button on the top side by passing the needle through all the layers and connecting another button on the underside. Come back through all the layers and pull the thread firmly through both buttons and all the layers of the fabric. Pull the buttons down to give a 'puffy' effect and then secure the thread.

tied quilting

button quilting

QUILTING IN PATTERNS Motifs can be made in many different shapes such as flowers, shells, scallops. This type of quilting is done in large negative spaces for added interest or on borders. Motifs can be used singly or for repeat designs. This type of pattern lends itself to trapunto quilting as well. (See page 169 for templates.)

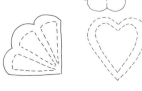

quilting motifs

Larger silk flowers can be attached with beads and used to decorate T-shirts and tops.

FREE-FORM PETALS are made by stitching two shapes together, turning through and attaching to the appliqué.

With right sides together, machine straight stitch the shapes together, leaving a small opening for turning through. Trim the seam allowance, clip any curves and turn through. Now lightly stuff the shapes. Top quilting can be added to give the petals definition.

Attach the petals to the background and satin stitch in place, closing the opening at the same time.

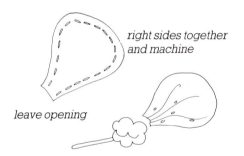

right sides together and machine

leave opening

clip curves, turn through and stuff

THREE-DIMENSIONAL PETALS These petals are made from suede or soft leather and are attached to garments.

Using the pattern on page 173, cut out five petals and a circle for the centre of the flower. Take a double thread and string the five petals onto it. Pull up the thread tightly, gathering the petals to form a circle. End off with a strong back stitch.

Run a gathering thread around the edge of the suede or leather circle and pull up, inserting a piece of batting as you tighten the circle so that it resembles a stuffed button. Attach the ring of petals to the back of the stuffed centre with whip stitches. Decorate the centre with beads, if desired.

A small piece of Velcro can be stitched to the back of the flower and to the garment so that the flower can be removed before washing.

BEADS AND SEQUINS

Beads and sequins can add glamour and dazzle to appliquéd garments or, for a more subtle effect, use beads in combination with appliqué. (See eyes of the Goosander chicks on page 66.)

The selection of beads available is fantastic, ranging from tiny glass beads, rhinestones and clay beads to carved, wooden beads. For appliqué, I would recommend the following three basic types:

▶ Tiny glass beads in a variety of colours both opaque and transparent

▶ Bugle beads in various lengths and colours

▶ Sequins in different shapes and sizes

BEADS should be placed neatly together in a pre-arranged order. A very long, thin needle with a tiny eye is a must. Choose the thread colour to suit your article and use a double thread, beginning and ending with a knot and a back stitch for extra strength.

INDIVIDUAL BEADS To attach individual beads, bring the needle through the fabric, thread the bead onto it and pull through. Insert the needle next to the first exit and make a stitch slightly longer than the bead with the thread below the needle. Pull through.

The bead details were worked to give added interest to the centre of this double vilene appliqué design. On completion, the beaded appliqué was then hand-hemmed onto the ground fabric.

Rose featuring free-form petals.

Notice the use of basic techniques and clever adaptations.

Individual, large beads can also be attached with a tiny seed bead.

SEEDING (crusting) Bring the needle through the fabric and thread three tiny beads onto it. Re-insert the needle into the fabric so that one bead rests on top of the other two.

COUCHING BEADS Bring the needle through the fabric, thread a number of beads onto the needle and pull the thread through. Position the first bead on the ground fabric and with a separate needle and thread make a holding stitch close to the bead, over the first thread. Slide the second bead up to the first and continue couching the thread between each bead.

An alternative method of couching is to thread a number of beads, the length of the space, onto the thread (like a necklace). Anchor this string of beads at the end with a back stitch, then come back over the 'necklace' catching the thread down between every second or third bead.
(See Ndebele Artist on page 90.)

DANGLING BEADS Secure the thread to the background and thread three bugle beads and one tiny bead onto it. Then re-insert the needle through the bugle beads using the tiny bead as the anchor. Secure the thread to the background. The lengths can vary depending on the number of bugle beads used.

Beads provide the perfect finish for this frog appliqué. The seeding gives a more raised effect and a different texture from the sequins. Many tiny beads are used which can make the work very heavy. Do not cover too large an area with this seeding technique.

SEQUINS There are a number of different methods of attaching sequins. Here are four examples:

SINGLE BACK STITCH Bring the needle through the fabric and sequin. Hold the sequin in position and make a back stitch over the right side of the sequin. Bring the needle up again to the left of the sequin, leaving enough space for the next sequin to fit edge to edge with the first.

DOUBLE BACK STITCH Bring the thread through the fabric and sequin. Make a back stitch over the right side of the sequin, then bring the needle out at the left of the sequin and make a second back stitch through the eye of the sequin. Bring the needle through the fabric leaving sufficient space for the next sequin.

WITH BEADS Bring the needle through the fabric and sequin. Thread a tiny seed bead onto the needle and insert the needle back through the eye of the sequin, pulling the thread tightly so that the tiny bead secures the sequin to the fabric.

INVISIBLE SEQUIN STITCH Bring the needle through the fabric and sequin. Make a small stitch to the left over the sequin into the fabric. Come back through the fabric leaving a small space half the size of the sequin. Thread on the second sequin and once again make a small stitch to the left, over the sequin and into the fabric. The second sequin must overlap the first so that the rim covers the thread and the eye of the previous sequin.

This appliqué combines ribbon, looping foot and bead details. The dangling beads create delightful tail feathers that swing free when the garment is worn.

Use the different sequin techniques and create a charming butterfly on a mohair jersey.

Be adventurous and combine a variety of beads and sequins to create different effects.

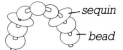 

bugle   bead   sequin

The beads on the silk flowers are both decorative and functional. The centre beads secure the petals to the garment.

This wall hanging has been machine outline quilted, that is, the diamond shapes are delineated by small stitches made 5 mm away from the patch. These stitches secure the three layers together and give added dimension.

QUILTING TECHNIQUES

There are a number of different quilting techniques which range from high relief (trapunto) to merely the suggestion of quilted rhythms (such as echo quilting and twin-needling). Appliqué and patchwork are both enhanced by quilting.

Here trapunto and echo quilting have been embellished with embroidery details.

Quilting is both functional, in that it provides warmth, and decorative. The quilting stitches hold the batting (wadding) in place and keep it from bunching. Stitches either follow the outlines of shapes in the design or they create decorative patterns on the background. Quilting can be done by hand with small running stitches or by machine.

BASIC REQUIREMENTS The following items are required for successful quilting:

Polyester *batting* (wadding) in large sheets

Polyester *stuffing* for trapunto or stuffed shapes

A quilting *hoop* or ring to hold the layers taut for hand quilting.

Quilting *thread* (number 50) This is a fairly thick thread that has been waxed. If it is not available, two strands of embroidery thread can be used instead.

Dressmaker's chalk/pencil, water soluble quilting pen or soft lead pencil to transfer the quilting design. If you use a pencil, press very lightly and make dotted rather than solid lines.

Cardboard for making templates if a motif is repeated or for intricate patterns.

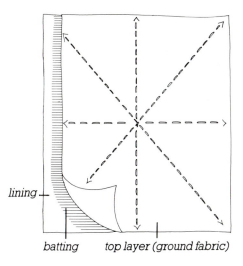

lining

batting   top layer (ground fabric)

Before you begin quilting, tack the three layers together; first the lining, wrong side up, then the batting and finally the appliqué or patchwork, right side up. Tack from the centre out towards each of the corners.

Begin quilting in the centre with tiny running stitches or machine stitching, working outwards to prevent puckering. If a quilt is made up of many designs, it is easier to work on small sections. For example, work each patchwork or appliqué block separately and then join them together to form the completed quilt or wall hanging.

As there are several quilting techniques to choose from, it is important to select one that will enhance the appliqué or patchwork. The following are some of the quilting methods available.

DIAGONAL QUILTING Stitch diagonal lines at regular intervals across the top of the quilt in one direction and then at the same intervals in the opposite direction to form a diamond pattern.

This cushion has been diagonal quilted by hand.

This quilt has been diagonal quilted by machine – notice the diamond pattern.

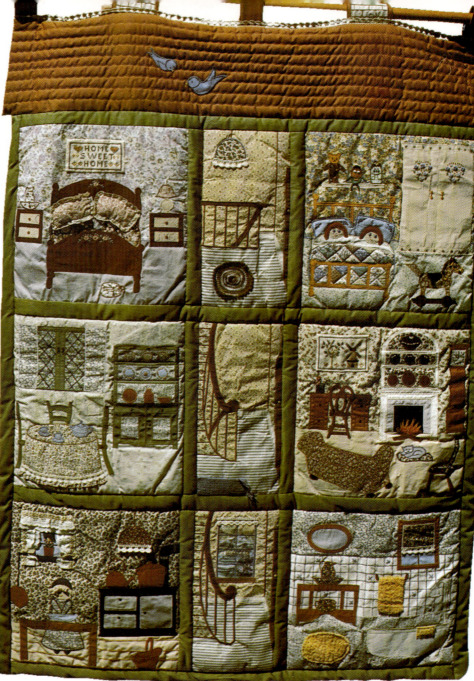

Each room of the doll's house was appliquéd and quilted, joined two rooms at a time and then row by row until the wall hanging was complete.

TIED AND BUTTONED QUILTING Another method of sewing the patchwork, batting and lining together is called tied quilting. This method is best if wool batting is used in place of polyester, as it is generally too thick for conventional quilting. The three layers are knotted together at regular intervals but although quicker, this method is not as decorative as stitched quilting.

Use an embroidery needle and wool or embroidery thread and make one stitch through all the layers, leaving a long end on top of the quilt. Make a back stitch and bring the needle up to the top again. Tie the ends together into a strong knot or tight bow.

Buttons can also be used to create a quilted effect. Secure a button on the top side by passing the needle through all the layers and connecting another button on the underside. Come back through all the layers and pull the thread firmly through both buttons and all the layers of the fabric. Pull the buttons down to give a 'puffy' effect and then secure the thread.

tied quilting

button quilting

QUILTING IN PATTERNS Motifs can be made in many different shapes such as flowers, shells, scallops. This type of quilting is done in large negative spaces for added interest or on borders. Motifs can be used singly or for repeat designs. This type of pattern lends itself to trapunto quilting as well. (See page 169 for templates.)

quilting motifs

Although the fabric and thread are the same colour, the different levels of quilting create the images, and interesting shadows are cast by the high and low relief work.

TRAPUNTO or high-relief quilting is an attractive form of quilting where selected areas of the design are padded to give a raised effect.

Cut a piece of background fabric and a corresponding piece of muslin. Put them together with the right side of the background fabric on top and transfer the quilting design onto the fabric using a dressmaker's pencil. Secure the two fabrics in a quilting hoop and stitch along the design lines in either back stitch or running stitch, making your stitches small and even.

With a small, sharp pair of scissors, make a small slit in the centre of each shape to be padded, or push the weave aside, and insert small pieces of polyester stuffing through the slit with the point of a knitting needle or crochet hook until the shape is evenly padded on the right side but not too hard. Some areas can be padded more than others to create different effects.

Sew up the slit with tiny whip stitches.

Trapunto is complemented by background quilting such as *echo quilting* (page 39) or *French knotting* (page 28) at regular intervals.

ECHO QUILTING This is a simple method of quilting by echoing the outlines of the trapunto, appliqué or patchwork shape.

To create echo quilting by *machine*, position the foot next to the appliqué, trapunto or patch and straight stitch around the designs using the foot space as your guide. Continue quilting until the entire background is patterned.

Hand echo quilting can be made at irregular intervals as shown on the cushion of *Trapunto daisies* (above). Remember to keep your stitches small and even.

To hand echo quilt or French knot the background (as shown in the *Trapunto nasturtiums*), cut a piece of flat batting and lining the same size as the trapunto fabric piece. Sandwich the batting between the top layers and the lining and tack. Quilt through all the layers using tiny running stitches (for echo) or French knots, moving from the trapunto design outwards.

CORDED QUILTING Sometimes called Italian quilting, this type of quilting gives an attractive raised effect which is suitable for linear patterns.

After transferring the design onto the fabric, tack the top and backing fabric (muslin) together with diagonal, vertical or horizontal lines. Machine straight stitch, or stitch by hand using back stitches or running stitches, along the parallel lines.

corded quilting

Working from the back and using a blunt bodkin or tapestry needle threaded with quilting wool or cord, insert the needle between the parallel lines.

To tie the cord off, make a small back stitch into the backing fabric (lining) or if the cord exits close to the beginning, knot the two ends of cord together. Do not pull the cord (wool) too tight; leave a little slack in case of shrinkage when the item is washed.

Notice the French knot quilting on the background fabric. Corded quilting has been used for the stems of the nasturtiums.

EMBROIDERY AND QUILTING can also be combined successfully. Instead of running stitches, trapunto outlines can be embroidered with chain stitch or French knots (like candlewicking). French knots can be used to delineate the shapes which can then be stuffed.

TWIN-NEEDLING gives a very subtle quilted effect. This double needle fits onto all machines and in combination with different settings and cams is excellent for creating many images, for example roof tops, wheat fields, pin-tucking on clothes, waves, clouds and so on.

The embroidery details are a few shades darker than the trapunto shapes and accent the feather patterns on the birds.

Notice the French knot quilting on the background fabric.

Twin-needle stitching gives an added dimension and exciting rhythms to a large background area.

This is a superb example of the many techniques described in this book.

FINISHING OFF

A good way to finish off quilts and wall hangings is to bind the edges with ready-made or self-fabric *bias binding*. Cut strips of fabric, on the cross, at least 4 cm wide. Tack the bias binding along the edge of the quilt or wall hanging, with right sides together, and machine straight stitch. Turn the binding over the edge, tuck under a small seam allowance and blind hem-stitch it in place.

Another method of binding is to cut the *lining* or ground fabric approximately 4 cm larger all round than the finished quilt or hanging. Roll the excess over and blind hem-stitch it in place. Mitre the corners for a professional finish.

A *ruffle* or frill and lining is a pretty and feminine way of finishing a quilt. Measure the border lengths of the quilt and cut the frill twice this length. Use a gathering stitch on the machine to sew two lines of stitches just inside the edge. Pull up the gathering threads and fit the ruffle to the quilt top, with right sides together, and machine stitch in place. Position the lining over the quilt top and ruffle and machine stitch, leaving a small opening for turning through. After turning through, close the opening with slip stitches.

To finish off patchwork quilts that have been *tied or buttoned* quilted, fold the lining and top fabric inwards and close with hand hemming or machine top stitching.

This Log Cabin patchwork has been quilted by stitching on the seams to form radiating squares.

The frill on this magnificent quilt adds olde worlde charm to the design and is a perfect match for the antique bed.

This is a very large wall hanging which is finished off with a small bias edge and topped with ribbon and lace.

PART THREE
DESIGN PROJECTS

A fun way to cheer up a simple garment.

MATERIALS

25 cm firm red, black or white cotton
small scraps of glamorous fabrics for
     butterflies or flowers
25 cm stiff iron-on vilene
contrasting and matching machine
     thread
seed beads
sequins
pearls
black and gold embroidery thread
gold metallic embroidery thread
red, yellow and blue embroidery thread
1 m x 1 cm wide each red, blue and
     yellow satin ribbon (for white belt)
3 m x 1 cm wide red satin ribbon (for
     red belt)

For patchwork belt

small scraps of nappa leather in navy
     blue, yellow, white, green and red
1 long strip black leather for lining of belt
matching machine thread

STITCHES USED

chain stitch (page 28)
twin-needle stitching (page 40)
satin stitch (page 29)
spider's web (page 28)

TEMPLATES

butterfly (page 132)
flower (page 132)
belt (page 172)

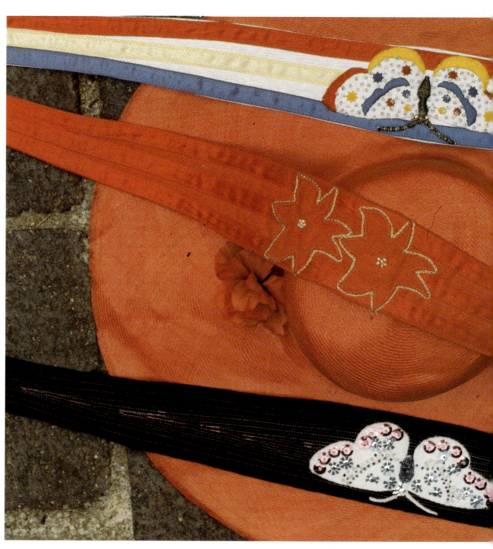

▶ Trace, cut and prepare the butterflies and flowers for the *Double vilene technique* on page 22.

BUTTERFLY BLACK BELT

▶ Enlarge the belt pattern and trace it onto the shiny side of the vilene. Iron it onto the wrong side of the black fabric.

▶ Fold the black fabric in half and cut out two belts, remembering to add a 6 mm seam allowance around the vilene. With right sides together, machine straight stitch the two pieces together, leaving a small opening for turning through.

▶ Turn through and decorate with twin-needle stitching in turquoise and pink thread.

▶ Bead the butterfly with turquoise and shocking pink sequins and seed beads.

▶ Hand hem the butterfly in place and embroider the feelers in satin stitch.

BUTTERFLY WHITE BELT

▶ Follow the instructions given above for preparing the butterfly and making the belt. Machine straight stitch the bands of red, blue and yellow satin ribbon onto the white belt. Make a ribbon tie by allowing the red ribbon to extend at each end of the belt to suit the waist size.

▶ Embroider the appliquéd butterfly with spider's webs and satin stitch. Dot with tiny, multi-coloured beads.

▶ Embroider the feelers and abdomen in satin stitch using black and gold embroidery thread.

▶ Hand hem the butterfly in position on the belt.

WORK BELTS

RED FLOWER BELT

▶ Follow the instructions given above on how to make the belt.

▶ Accent the flowers by chain stitching in gold metallic thread. Crust a few baby pearls in the centre and then hand hem the flowers onto the belt.

PATCHWORK BELT

▶ Enlarge the pattern of the belt by following the instructions on page 18 and cut it out of black leather.

▶ Trace the design on the belt pattern and make your own templates for the leather patches. These pieces only need a 6 mm seam allowance where two colours will meet. Glue the patches in place on the black belt.

▶ Straight stitch each patch in matching machine thread. Punch holes in the belt and attach a smart buckle. The belt is fully reversible if black thread is used in the bobbin.

RIBBON BAG

MATERIALS

50 cm white feather leather
50 cm cotton lining in matching or
  contrasting colour
matching machine thread for ribbons
white machine thread
1 m ribbon in each colour
2 m drawstring

This is a bag for all seasons. The basic pattern is simple and can be appliquéd or patched with ribbon, lace, leather or chintz. Geometric, floral and abstract designs are ideal.

▶ Cut out the following pieces in both feather leather and lining:
  80 cm x 35 cm for sides*
  23 cm diameter circle for the base
  80 cm x 6 cm strap

▶ Cut the ribbon lengths to fit the basic rectangle of the bag. The ribbon can be arranged in parallel lines, or in woven or zigzag patterns.

▶ Machine zigzag the ribbons in place with matching machine thread.

▶ With right sides together, join the short sides of the rectangle to form a cylinder.

▶ Pleat the cylinder to fit the base and, with right sides facing, stitch them together.

▶ Make the lining in the same way, slip it into the bag, wrong sides together, and catch the two bases together with a few back stitches. Fold the top edges in and top stitch.

▶ Cut two 38 cm x 3 cm wide strips of feather leather or ribbon for the drawstring gusset. Attach the strips 3 cm down from the top edge, on the outside of the bag, leaving the ends of the strips open.

▶ Cut the drawstring in half. Using a safety-pin and beginning at one side, thread one cord right around the bag and exit on the same side. Begin at the opposite side with the other piece of cord, threading it in the same way. Knot the ends of each cord together and pull up.

▶ With right sides together, join the strap and its lining, leaving a small opening for pulling through. Pull through and sew up the opening by top stitching. Sew the strap inside the bag on opposite sides at the drawstring exits.

*NOTE Cut the sides 80 cm x 40 cm if a deeper bag is required.

This design is delightful on a T-shirt. Without the beads, it also makes an ideal appliqué on guest towels or on a tablecloth.

GLITTERING FROG

MATERIALS
25 cm white chintz for lilies
25 cm green chintz for frog and leaves
50 cm iron-on vilene
white and green machine thread
green sequins in various sizes and shapes
seed beads in white, yellow and shades
   of green
1 yellow rhinestone for the eye

TEMPLATE
frog and lilies (page 158)

▶ Enlarge the design by following the instructions on page 18.

▶ Trace, cut and prepare the frog and waterlilies for the *Double vilene technique* on page 23.

▶ Machine satin stitch the frog outlines and linear details in corresponding thread. Do not cut away the excess vilene before beading.

▶ Referring to the photograph for details, sequin the frog's body, securing the sequins with a tiny seed bead. Crust the

eye surround using three baby beads at a time. Couch (page 36) the seed beads onto the chest and limb extremities.

▶ Couch the seed beads on the diagonal to create the details on the waterlilies.

▶ Once the beading is complete, cut away the excess vilene.

▶ Place the designs on the T-shirt and blind hem-stitch them in position. Make small clusters of yellow beads on the background of the T-shirt.

BIG SQUARES

This delightful single bed quilt is a machine pieced, simple patchwork with a contemporary appeal.

MATERIALS
white, pink and lilac shades of poly-
   cotton*
3 m polyester batting
3 m plain poly-cotton for lining
pink machine thread

TEMPLATE
20 cm x 20 cm square (page 117)

▶ Make a 20 cm x 20 cm cardboard template. This includes your seam allowance and finished squares must measure 18 cm x 18 cm. This quilt is made up of 8 squares across by 13 squares down. Cut 104 squares in an interesting balance of light and dark colours. Machine piece the patchwork together in rows of eight squares across. Press the seams open and flat.

*NOTE The quantities of fabric required will depend on the size of the bed and the width of the fabric.

▶ Machine piece four rows of eight squares, taking care while sewing as each block must line up precisely.

▶ Begin quilting at this point. Cut the polyester batting the size of the patchwork and baste on the diagonal.

▶ Using a quilting foot, straight stitch on the junction of all the squares up to 1 cm from the edge where the next pieced block of four rows will be attached.

▶ Piece and quilt the next set of four rows. Join this section to the first section, right sides together.

▶ Whip stitch the batting together and quilt the seam line on the right side.

▶ Join the last five rows and attach to the previously quilted section. Quilt, whip stitch the batting together and quilt along the block junction.

▶ The border is made up of three bands of colour. Cut two 236 cm x 5 cm wide strips and two 154 cm x 5 cm wide strips in the first colour. The seam allowance is 1 cm on each side with the finished width being 3 cm.

▶ Attach the longer strips first and fold them outwards. Attach the shorter strips.

▶ Cut two 244 cm x 5 cm wide strips and two 162 cm x 5 cm wide strips in the second colour, attach them and fold them outwards in the same way.

▶ Cut two 252 cm x 10 cm strips and two 170 cm x 10 cm strips in the third colour. This strip is double the width because it forms the rolled border. Attach these pieces in the same way.

▶ Cut lengths of polyester batting 10 cm wide and baste onto the border.

▶ Machine quilt in the seam junctions. Whip the border batting to the patchwork top batting on the underside.

▶ Cut the lining 5 cm smaller than the bordered quilt. Baste the lining in place and roll the border over the raw edge of the lining.

▶ Hand hem or open zigzag the border to the lining. The lining can be caught at intervals to the top if necessary by using tied or buttoned quilting to give a more 'puffy' finish. This will make the quilt stronger and the reverse side will be very attractive. I would recommend this extra quilting if a very large quilt is being made (see *Quilting* on page 37).

BABY BLOCKS

This delightful patchwork is perfect for a baby's antique high chair. This design would be equally charming on a cot quilt or pram cover.

MATERIALS
25 cm olive green cotton
25 cm white cotton
50 cm floral sprigged cotton
50 cm calico for lining
polyester stuffing
matching machine thread

TEMPLATES
diamonds and triangles (page 116)

▶ Cut out nine diamonds in green, eight in floral and nine in white.

▶ Cut two half diamonds in floral, two triangles in white and two in floral and two half triangles in white and two in floral.

▶ Machine or hand stitch a floral diamond to a green diamond, then join a white diamond to the floral and green diamonds. Take care when piecing together as the corners must meet exactly. Make up eight of these three-dimensional blocks.

▶ Join three blocks for the first row.

▶ For the second row, piece a white diamond to the green diamond of a completed block and a floral half diamond to the white diamond. Then piece a completed block to the first completed block, a dark green diamond to the white diamond of the second block and a floral half diamond to the green diamond.

▶ Piece three blocks together for the third row.

▶ Join the three rows together and fill in the gaps with floral triangles and half triangles at the bottom and white triangles and half triangles along the top.

▶ Cut four 33 cm x 3 cm wide green strips for the frame and machine straight stitch the top and bottom strips first and then add the side strips. Press open the seams.

▶ Cut out two 40 cm x 25 cm floral pieces for the backing and turn a hem under one long edge of each piece. With right sides together, stitch the back pieces to the patchwork front. Trim, clip corners, overlock and turn through.

▶ For the cushion, cut two 40 cm x 40 cm pieces of calico and machine together, leaving a small opening. Turn through and fill with polyester stuffing. Sew up the opening with neat whip stitches.

JACOB'S LADDER

This is a good beginner's block. It consists of nine pieced squares; five of the squares each being made up of four smaller squares with the remaining four squares each being made up of two triangles.

MATERIALS
50 cm cream cotton
25 cm cream and beige sprigged
    cotton
25 cm mix 'n match beige sprigged
    cotton
50 cm calico
small packet of polyester stuffing
matching machine thread

TEMPLATES
squares and diamonds (page 123)

▶ Cut ten squares in cream; ten squares in the sprigged cotton; four triangles in cream and four in the mix 'n match sprigged cotton.

▶ Machine piece two plain and two patterned squares to make up a block. Make five blocks in this way.

▶ Piece a plain and a patterned triangle to make up a block. Make four blocks in this way.

▶ Using the diagram on page 123, join a square block, double triangle block and a square block to form the first row.

▶ For the second row, join a double triangle block, a square block and a double triangle block.

▶ Repeat the arrangement of the first row to form the third row.

▶ Join the rows, making sure the blocks are in line.

▶ Cut a 264 cm x 10 cm strip of cream and beige sprigged cotton for the frill. Fold the strip in half and machine two rows of gathering stitches along the raw edges.

▶ Cut two 34 cm x 25 cm pieces of cream cotton for the backing and turn under a hem along one long side of each piece.

▶ Tack the frill to the right side of the patchwork so that it is folded inwards, place the right sides of the backing

fabric facing the patchwork and machine the front and back pieces together. Clip corners, trim, overlock and turn through.

▶ Cut two 34 cm x 34 cm pieces of calico for the inside cushion, and machine together leaving a small opening for turning through. Clip corners, trim and turn through. Fill with polyester stuffing and sew up the opening with slip stitches. Slip the cushion into the finished patchwork cover.

TINY TOTS

MATERIALS
scraps of gaily coloured cottons (plain,
    sprigged, spotted and geometric)
iron-on vilene
matching machine thread
selection of embroidery thread

TEMPLATES
flower and bee (page 129)
crocodile (page 129)
toadstool (page 128)
house (page 127)
apple (page 127)
dress and dungarees (page 174)

▶ Cut out the yokes and pockets. It is
easier to appliqué the designs *directly*
onto the fabric before the garment is
made up.

▶ Trace, cut and prepare the designs for
the *Direct appliqué technique* on page
21. Do not forget underlap seam
allowances where two raw edges meet.

▶ Cut out, position and tack the shapes
onto the background fabric. Machine
satin stitch in place.

▶ Add any embroidery details, such as
bees, butterflies or little flowers that might
add to the charm of the garment (see
Embroidery stitches pages 28-29).

▶ Make up the dress or dungarees.

*These cute little designs are quite
charming for toddlers' pockets or
yokes on dungarees or dresses. The
patterns for the dress and dungarees
can be found on page 174.*

PRAM COVER

The little pram cover design was adapted from a piece of wrapping paper and the cot quilt was a lovely way of using the left over scraps from the duck appliqué.

MATERIALS

75 cm yellow gingham for lining and border
50 cm plain blue cotton for sky
25 cm striped blue and white cotton for the water
25 cm pale yellow for the ducks
small scraps:
   red and navy geometrics for hats
   bright yellow for the beaks and fish
   patterned yellow for the little wings
   primary coloured geometrics for fish
84 cm x 67 cm polyester batting
iron-on vilene
matching machine thread
black, white, red, green and silver embroidery thread

STITCHES USED

satin stitch (page 29)
spider's web (page 28)
raised chain stitch (page 29)
chain stitch (page 28)
buttonhole bar (page 28)
bullion rosebuds (page 28)
saddle stitch

TEMPLATE

ducks (page 172)

▶ Enlarge the design by following the instructions on page 18.

▶ Prepare the ducks, sky, fish and water for *Direct appliqué* (page 21).

▶ Tack the entire design together and machine satin stitch in matching colours.

▶ Embroider the duck's eyes in black, blue and white spider's webs; the fishing rod is red raised chain, black chain and a silver buttonhole bar; the fishes' eyes in black spider's webs and the bubbles in green bullion rosebuds. Saddle stitch the hat brim in white and satin stitch a blue bow on the other hat.

▶ Cut a 84 cm x 67 cm piece of gingham lining. Sandwich the batting between the appliqué and the lining and tack on the diagonals.

▶ Wrap the gingham lining around to meet the appliqué, folding the excess batting in half to form the 5 cm wide border, and make a 1 cm turn under.

▶ Mitre the corners, tack and machine zigzag through all the layers.

COT QUILT

This quilt is made up entirely from scraps. The finished size is 115 cm x 72 cm.

▶ Using scraps of different lengths, make up seven 106 cm x 9 cm strips, seam allowances included.

▶ Join the strips to form the finished patchwork top.

▶ Cut a 115 cm x 72 cm piece of batting and a 125 cm x 82 cm piece of yellow cotton for the lining and border.

▶ Sandwich the batting between the patchwork and the lining. Bring the lining around to meet the patchwork, folding the batting in half to form a border. Make a 1 cm turn under on the lining, then tack and machine zigzag through all the layers.

▶ The individual patches can also be quilted for more definition. Quilting is always done from the centre outwards, so if this effect is required, quilt the patches first and then finish with the border.

EIGHT POINT STAR

This is a very popular star pattern and the block repeated makes a stunning quilt. It is also very effective as a Christmas star in green, red and white. The optical vibrations are dynamic if the star is pieced in two colours but many different colours can also be combined successfully.

MATERIALS
50 cm navy polyester cotton
25 cm red polyester cotton
25 cm patterned polyester cotton
50 cm calico
polyester stuffing
matching machine thread
1 card red piped bias binding

TEMPLATES
diamonds and squares (page 121)

▶ Cut out four diamonds in red and four in pattern; four squares and four triangles in navy.

▶ Machine or hand stitch the red and patterned diamonds together in pairs, then join two pairs to create a straight base as shown on page 121. Follow the photograph for the colour sequence.

▶ Join the two pieces of four diamonds together, making sure the lines are straight and that the points of the star are not lost in the seam allowance.

▶ Stitch the navy triangles and squares in position to complete the 30 cm square block.

▶ Now cut two 31 cm x 3,5 cm wide strips and two 36 cm x 3,5 cm wide strips in red (seam allowance included). Cut two 36 cm x 4,5 cm wide strips and two 45 cm x 4,5 cm wide strips in navy (seam allowances included). Attach them to form the border.

▶ Cut two 45 cm x 30 cm pieces of navy cotton and turn over a hem along one long edge of each piece. Position the red piped bias binding on top of the patchwork and cover with the navy backing, wrong side up. Machine stitch around the cushion, clip corners, trim and turn through.

▶ Cut two 45 cm x 45 cm pieces of calico and machine stitch together, leaving a small opening for the stuffing. Turn through and stuff with polyester stuffing. Sew up the opening with tiny whip stitches.

▶ Insert the calico cushion into the patchwork cover and sew up the opening with tiny hem-stitches.

PLACE MATS

MATERIALS*
10 cm each of ten fabrics in different
    colours
38 cm x 30 cm batting
39 cm x 31 cm white lining
white machine thread
2 m x 5 cm wide white cotton lace

▶ Make an 8,5 cm x 8,5 cm template
and cut out two fabric squares from
each colour.

▶ Arrange the colours at random and
join five squares together using a 5 mm
seam allowance. Iron the seams open
and flat.

▶ Make three more rows of five squares
each.

▶ Sew the four rows together to create the
completed mat.

▶ Tack the batting to the patchwork and
machine quilt on the seams.

▶ With right sides together, pin and tack
the lace to the edges, easing it slightly at
the corners.

▶ With right sides together (lining right
side up, then the lace, then the
patchwork right side down), machine
stitch around the place mat leaving a
small opening for turning through. Clip
the corners, trim and turn through. Sew
up the opening with tiny slip stitches.

*This is a quick and easy patchwork
that is ideal for beginners.*

*NOTE These measurements are for
one place mat. Use 10 different
colours of fabric and cut out two
squares per colour. The seam allowance is included in the measurements.

COUNTRY CUSHIONS

MATERIALS for Dresden plate cushion
25 cm each of three mix 'n match
 burgundy and blue sprigged cottons
50 cm plain burgundy cotton
50 cm calico
polyester stuffing
matching machine thread

TEMPLATE
Dresden plate (page 120)

▶ Cut out one small circle, using the template provided, and two 40 cm diameter circles from the plain burgundy cotton.

▶ Cut out three Dresden plate panels from each of the three sprigged mix 'n match fabrics.

▶ Join the nine panels to form a circular, floral shape.

▶ Whip the centre circle to the sprigged panels, then place the pieced panels onto a large burgundy circle and hand hem the design onto the background, turning under the seam allowances and clipping curves if necessary.

▶ Measure the circumference of the large burgundy circle. Cut out a 12 cm wide strip, double that circumference, of plain fabric and a 8 cm wide strip, double that circumference, of sprigged fabric.

▶ Fold each strip in half and machine stitch two rows of gathering stitch along each raw edge. Gather the fabric strips to form two frills.

▶ Machine stitch the frills to the right side of the patchwork and place the second burgundy circle on top. Machine stitch around the cushion, leaving a 15 cm opening for turning through and inserting the inside cushion.

▶ Cut two 40 cm diameter circles from calico and machine stitch together, leaving a small opening for turning through.

▶ Turn through and stuff the calico cushion with polyester stuffing. Sew up the opening with tiny whip stitches and insert the cushion into the patchwork cover. Sew the backing to the frill using tiny slip stitches.

MATERIALS for triangle cushion
25 cm plain burgundy cotton
25 cm pink and blue sprigged cotton
40 cm x 40 cm pink cotton
40 cm x 40 cm calico
polyester stuffing
matching machine thread

TEMPLATE
triangle (page 120)

This is a quick and easy patchwork which can be machine pieced. A successful design is achieved using plain and sprigged fabrics arranged on the diagonal.

▶ Cut out nine triangles from the sprigged fabric and nine from the plain.

▶ Join the triangles (a plain and a sprigged) in pairs to make nine squares.

▶ Machine stitch the squares in rows, referring to the photograph for the placement of the colours. The joining of the rows must be accurate to give perfect corners.

▶ Cut out two 38 cm x 2 cm wide strips and two 40 cm x 2 cm wide strips from the plain burgundy fabric and machine stitch them to the patchwork to form a border.

▶ With right sides together, machine stitch the pink backing to the patchwork front, leaving one side open for turning through and inserting the cushion.

▶ Machine stitch together the two calico squares, leaving a small opening for turning through.

▶ Turn through and fill with polyester stuffing. Sew up the opening with tiny whip stitches.

▶ Insert the cushion into the patchwork cover and sew up the opening with tiny slip stitches.

MATERIALS for Log Cabin cushion
25 cm each of three different pink
 sprigged cottons
25 cm each of three different navy
 sprigged cottons
25 cm navy cotton
25 cm calico
polyester stuffing
matching machine thread

TEMPLATE
log cabin (pages 118-119)

This design can be pieced very
successfully by machine.

▶ Using the templates provided, cut the
strips from the navy and pink sprigged
cotton and a centre square from the
navy cotton. Arrange the 14 light and
14 dark strips as desired around the
centre square. Follow the instructions on
page 13 for machine stitching the strips
into position. The finished block is
34 cm square (seam allowances
included).

▶ Cut out a 34 cm x 34 cm piece of navy
cotton and with right sides together,
machine stitch it to the patchwork,
leaving one side open for turning through
and inserting the inside cushion.

▶ Cut two 34 cm x 34 cm pieces of
calico and machine stitch together,
leaving a small opening for turning
through.

▶ Turn through and fill with polyester
stuffing. Sew up the opening with tiny
whip stitches.

▶ Insert the cushion into the patchwork
cover and sew up the opening with tiny
slip stitches.

*These subdued colours look wonderful
on a cream background in an old-
fashioned setting or, in total contrast,
on modern leather furniture.*

FREYDI'S QUILT

This traditional quilt uses the barn raising variation of Log Cabin patchwork.

▶ Begin by cutting a 5 cm x 5 cm burgundy square. Position the square in the centre of the calico, referring to page 12 for details.

▶ Using the templates as guides, cut out the 3 cm wide strips and, following the Log Cabin placement diagram on page 13, begin with the green strips and machine stitch them, with a 6 mm seam allowance, to the centre square. Press the seams open.

▶ Once you have made 60 blocks, join them in rows of six and then join the ten rows together to make up the complete patchwork top.

▶ Cut out the border strips and attach the long sides first. Press the seams towards the border.

▶ Now attach the two short border strips and press the seams as before.

▶ Place the batting between the patchwork top and the lining and tack the three layers together from the centre towards the sides.

▶ Using two strands of embroidery thread, hand quilt the centre burgundy medallion with tiny running stitches, working from the centre outwards through the intersecting corners to the edges. Continue until the centre medallion is quilted.

▶ Now hand quilt along the borders of the burgundy medallions to complete the quilting.

▶ Roll the border strips over to meet the lining and hand hem in place.

▶ If necessary, quilt just inside the rolled edge.

NOTE Each completed block measures about 23 cm square, with the quilt being made up of 60 blocks.

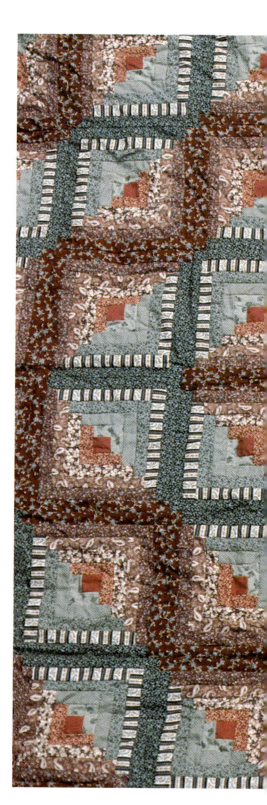

MATERIALS
For each block
5 green sprigged fabrics each used twice
5 burgundy sprigged fabrics each used twice
1 plain central burgundy square
23 cm x 23 cm calico
and
2 x 14 cm x 232 cm burgundy strips for the border
2 x 14 cm x 163 cm burgundy strips for the border
250 cm x 170 cm polyester batting
250 cm x 170 cm green or burgundy lining
burgundy and green machine thread
burgundy embroidery thread

TEMPLATES
Log Cabin (pages 118-119)

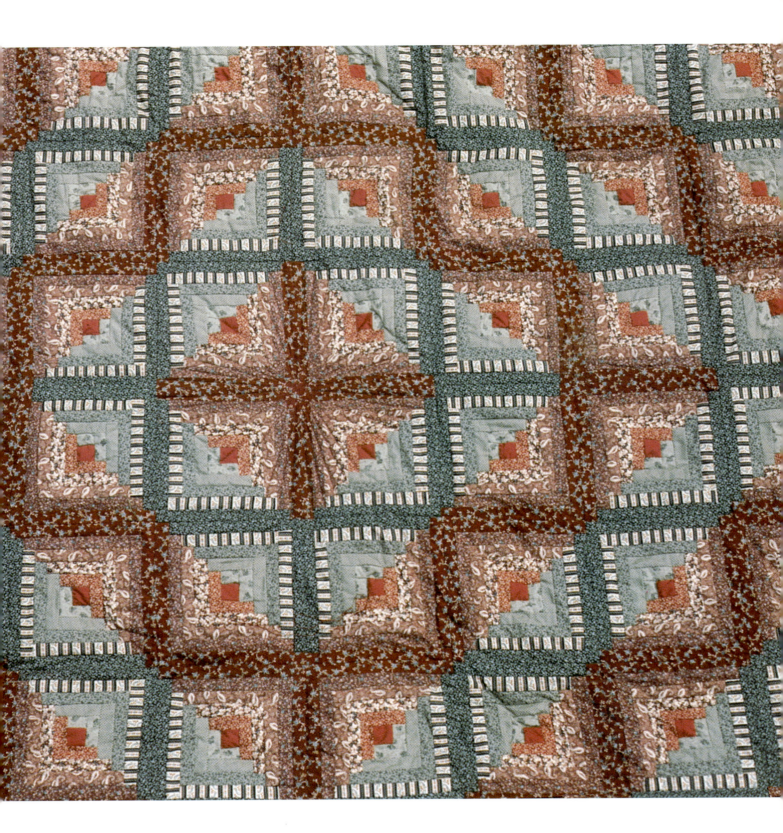

GOLFING RAT

This appliqué is a delightful interpretation of a greeting card. It makes an ideal gift for any golfing enthusiast.

MATERIALS
25 cm red T-shirt fabric for the jersey
25 cm tartan fabric for the pants
25 cm mohair fabric for face, hands and tail
small piece of contrasting fabric for inside ear
80 cm x 61 cm khaki cotton for background
small pieces of cotton for cap, collar and cuffs
soft leather for tackies
scraps of silver lamé, tan leather and raw silk for golf club and ball
iron-on vilene
matching machine thread
black and yellow embroidery thread
white, black, yellow and red ric-rac
1 red button
nylon thread
1 m very narrow yellow ribbon

STITCHES USED
satin stitch (page 29)
French knots (page 28)
spider's web (page 28)
bullion knots (page 28)
long stab stitches (page 78)

TEMPLATE
golfing rat (page 173)

▶ Enlarge the design by following the instructions on page 18. Prepare, cut and assemble all the pieces for *Direct appliqué* by following the instructions on page 21. Remember superimposed pieces do not require seam allowances but where the raw edges of two pieces meet, one edge must have an underlap allowance.

▶ Pin and tack all the shapes onto the background fabric and machine satin stitch in matching thread. Do not stitch the soles of the tackies.

▶ Tuck half the black ric-rac under the tackies to give the effect of ridged soles and machine satin stitch. Attach the rest of the ric-rac with an open zigzag stitch.

▶ Hand embroider the nose in satin stitch. For the whiskers make a black French knot, then pull two strands of gut through the knot, leaving a 1 cm end. Make a back stitch and come back through the French knot and cut off the gut leaving a 1 cm end again. Continue in this fashion.

▶ Make a black and yellow spider's web

on the ankle of one tackie, and bullion knots on both tackies to thread the laces through. Lace the narrow yellow ribbon under and over the bullion knots and then tie the ribbon as you would shoe laces. Complete the linear details on the shoes with long stab stitches.

▶ Stitch the red button to the cap.

TUMBLING PANDAS

These delightful fellows will cheer up any top. They are also charming on cot bumpers or as a wall hanging in a child's bedroom.

MATERIALS
small pieces of black and white cotton
iron-on vilene
matching machine thread
black, white, pink and red embroidery
  thread

STITCHES USED
stem stitch (page 28)
satin stitch (page 29)
spider's web (page 28)
French knots (page 28)

TEMPLATES
pandas (pages 143-145)

▶ Trace the pandas directly onto the iron-on vilene, *shiny-side up.*

▶ Iron the entire panda, with all its details, onto the white fabric.

▶ Trace the black shapes separately and superimpose these pieces onto the white panda.

▶ Using the *Double Vilene technique* on page 22, assemble the pandas on another piece of vilene, tack in position and machine satin stitch all the raw edges. Cut away the excess vilene.

▶ Hand embroider the details, using stem stitch on the outlines, satin stitch for the nose and tongue, spider's web for the eyes and French knots for the pads and toes.

▶ Attach the pandas to the garment with an open zigzag or straight stitch just inside the satin-stitched edge.

CIRCUS TRAIN

The versatility of appliqué images is well illustrated in the tumbling pandas which form a part of this circus train. The finishing touches are provided by sequins, ric-rac, buttons and bows. This design makes a delightful border on curtains.

MATERIALS

25 cm each of a selection of primary coloured cottons for the carriages
25 cm each spotted fabric for giraffe
25 cm each black and white chintz for pandas
50 cm pink cotton for elephants
small pieces brown cotton in variety of shades for lions and monkey
floral fabric for elephant's blanket
granny print for train wheels
iron-on vilene
1 m white cotton for background
matching machine thread
1 card yellow ric-rac
1 m green cord
1 m each red, blue and green narrow ribbon
6 buttons
shocking pink and green sequins
black, white and brown embroidery thread

STITCHES USED

bullion knots (page 28)
French knots (page 28)
spider's web (page 28)
satin stitch (page 29)
stem stitch (page 28)
back stitch (page 28)

TEMPLATE

circus train (pages 164-165)
panda (page 145)

▶ Enlarge the design by following the instructions on page 18.

▶ Trace, cut and prepare the elephant and carriages for *Direct appliqué* (page 21) and tack them onto the background fabric.

▶ Trace, cut and prepare the other animals (pandas, monkey, giraffe and lion family) for the *Double vilene technique* (page 22).

▶ Machine satin stitch the animals in matching machine thread and trim away the excess vilene.

▶ Hand embroider the face details with black, white and brown embroidery thread using bullion knots, French knots or spider's web for eyes, satin stitch for noses and mouth. Embroider linear detail in stem or back stitch.

▶ Tack the animals in their carriages and open zigzag them in place over the satin-stitched edge.

▶ Tack and machine straight stitch the ric-rac poles in position and then machine satin stitch all the carriages and the elephant directly onto the background.

▶ Attach the green cord, buttons and bows with blind hem-stitch and add the sequins to the elephant's headgear using invisible sequin stitch (page 36).

ON SAFARI

*This charming appliqué makes a
wonderful headboard or quilt for a
child's room. It would also provide a
humorous note to a family room or
private game lodge.*

MATERIALS

150 cm x 53 cm pale grey cotton or linen for the background sky
150 cm x 35 cm bright blue cotton for the river
150 cm x 35 cm cream cotton or linen for the foreground sand
75 cm brown cotton for the tree
25 cm bottle-green cotton for bushes and leaves
25 cm pale green anglaise for bushes and leaves
40 cm medium grey cotton for elephants, ciné camera, bumpers and grill on car and the driver's vest
50 cm brown velvet for the lions
40 cm red cotton for the jeep
small scraps:
    paisley for the snake; dark grey for the hippo; tartan for the seat covers; mustard and black cotton for wheels; geometric prints for the giraffe and crocodile; white and cream for the men; black velvet for the baboon
iron-on vilene
matching machine thread
50 cm brown cord
black, brown, yellow, white and pink embroidery thread
small length white ric-rac for crocodile's teeth
1 pink sequin and black seed bead for the snake's eye

STITCHES USED

bullion knots (page 28)
stem stitch (page 28)
spider's web (page 28)
satin stitch (page 29)
stab stitch (page 78)
bullion rosebuds (page 28)

TEMPLATE

safari scene (pages 164-165)

▶ Enlarge the design by following the instructions on page 18.

▶ Trace, cut and prepare the bushes, river and tree for *Direct appliqué* (page 21) onto the background. Tack all these pieces together and machine satin stitch to create one large working background.

▶ Following the instructions for the *Double vilene technique* on page 22, trace, cut and prepare the animals, men and jeep.

▶ Machine satin stitch each animal using the photograph as a guide for special effects and thread colours.

▶ Hand embroider the eyes, noses, whiskers and facial details of the lion family in light brown and yellow as follows: the eyes in bullions and the other details in stem stitch. Using the looping foot, machine the lion's mane in rows.

▶ Embroider the crocodile's eyes and nostrils in black and yellow spider's web. Zigzag the ric-rac in place for teeth.

▶ Satin stitch the hippo's tongue in pink and his teeth in white.

▶ Embroider the elephant's eyes in black and white satin stitch and the giraffe's eyes in green bullions with black stab stitch lashes.

▶ Bead the snake's eye and embroider yellow and white bullion eyes for the gorilla. Using the looping foot, machine hair on the men and hand embroider the eye details in satin stitch.

▶ Machine satin stitch together all the parts of the jeep and embroider black bullion rosebuds on the spare wheel to resemble screws.

▶ Hand hem or open zigzag all the parts onto the background fabric.

▶ Couch the brown cord in place as shown.

▶ The design can be framed as a headboard or quilted for a wall hanging or bed cover.

WATER BIRDS

These designs offer enormous scope for experimentation with textures. The birds can be used individually on cushions or garments or combined with lilies, rocks, frogs and bulrushes to make an enormous wall hanging.

MATERIALS
A selection of small pieces of patterned and textured velvets, towelling, satins suedes, textured silks and chintz
matching machine thread
embroidery thread
1 m soutache (cord)
tiny black beads

STITCHES USED
bullion knots (page 28)
buttonhole bars (page 28)
French knots (page 28)

TEMPLATES
duck and drake (page 166)
goosander and chicks (page 161)
heron (page 161)
bird in flight (page 161)
small blue bird with chicks (page 166)

▶ Enlarge the designs by following the instructions on page 18 and prepare each bird for the *Double vilene technique* as described on page 22. Refer to the photographs as you work for a guide to colour choice and stitch details.

▶ Hand embroider the eyes with bullion knots, buttonhole bars and French knots. Use tiny black beads for the chicks' eyes.

▶ Hand hem the finished birds onto cushions or onto a large background.

NOTE Rocks, water insects, frogs, fish and lilies can be added to the wall hanging with stunning results.
Be adventurous and use sheer fabrics to give the illusion of water.

EAGLE IN FLIGHT

This is a quick and easy double vilene appliqué that is ideal for a denim jacket or T-shirt.

MATERIALS
40 cm pale blue satin for main bird
23 cm dark blue satin for upper-wings
iron-on vilene
silver machine thread
silver and black embroidery thread
small packet silver sequins
small packet crystal seed beads
1 rhinestone for the eye

STITCHES USED
satin stitch (page 29)
French knots (page 28)
chain stitch (page 28)
bullion knots (page 28)

TEMPLATE
eagle (page 166)

▶ Enlarge the design by following the instructions on page 18.

▶ Trace the entire bird onto the shiny side of the iron-on vilene. Cut out and iron onto the pale blue satin.

▶ Trace the upper-wings, head and body onto the shiny side of the iron-on vilene. Cut out and iron onto the dark blue satin.

▶ Cut and tack the dark blue satin shape to the main bird.

▶ Cut out the bird, place it on a larger piece of vilene and machine satin stitch in silver thread as shown in the photograph.

▶ Bead the upper-wing with sequins held in place with a seed bead and stitch the rhinestone into position for the eye. Cut away the excess vilene.

▶ Hand hem the eagle onto the garment.

▶ Draw the claws and snake directly onto the garment. Machine or hand satin stitch the snake in silver and embroider the divisions on the body with black bullion knots. French knot the eye in black.

▶ Embroider the eagle's legs and claws in silver chain stitch.

BIRDS OF A FEATHER

Although the colours are subtle, the different wools, touch of coral embroidery and trapunto bamboo branches all provide an exciting third dimension.

MATERIALS
50 cm fine cream linen
50 cm muslin
4 balls exciting wools ranging from
  cream to beige
small piece heavily textured fabric for
  feeding dish
iron-on vilene
polyester stuffing
matching machine thread
cream, beige, coral and brown
  embroidery thread
black beads and tiny pearls

STITCHES USED
couching (page 29)
spider's web (page 28)
chain stitch (page 28)
French knots (page 28)
Pekinese stitch (page 28)
stab stitch (page 78)
bullion knots (page 28)

TEMPLATES
lovebirds (page 133)
parrot (page 155)

▶ Enlarge the design of the parrot. Trace the parrot and lovebirds onto iron-on vilene, *shiny-side down*.

▶ Cut out the birds on the outlines and iron them in position on the *right side* of the cream linen.

▶ Embroider the birds combining all the different embroidery stitches illustrated on pages 28-29. For the parrot, use couching for the head, spider's web for the eye, chain stitch and French knots for the beak, Pekinese stitch for the wings and stab stitch for the tail feathers. Embroider six-strand bullion knots for the claws. Embroider the lovebirds in a similar fashion.

▶ Trace the feeding dish onto iron-on vilene, *shiny-side up*. Iron onto the back of the heavily textured fabric and cut out, leaving a 5 mm seam allowance. Turn under the seam allowance, tack the dish onto the background fabric and hand hem it in place (for hand appliqué) or machine satin stitch in place, without seam allowances, if machine appliquéd.

▶ Embroider French knots on top of the dish using six strands of coral embroidery thread.

▶ Draw the bamboo branches on the linen with a dressmaker's pencil. Tack the muslin onto the back of the linen along the outer edges. Chain stitch the outlines of the bamboo with three strands of beige embroidery thread.

▶ Make a small slit into the muslin behind the branches and fill the cavities with stuffing (see *Trapunto quilting* page 39). Sew up the opening with tiny whip stitches.

▶ Embroider the knots in the bamboo with beige buttonhole bars.

▶ Attach a black bead to each eye, anchoring it with a tiny pearl.

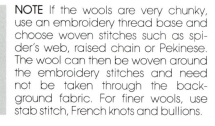

NOTE If the wools are very chunky, use an embroidery thread base and choose woven stitches such as spider's web, raised chain or Pekinese. The wool can then be woven around the embroidery stitches and need not be taken through the background fabric. For finer wools, use stab stitch, French knots and bullions.

FIGHTING COCKS

This design is created from appliquéd patches of leather and top stitched with metallic thread.

MATERIALS
Small pieces of leather, suede and
  snake skin in shades of blue, shocking
  pink, purple, white, yellow, red, green,
  bronze and black
2 rhinestones for the eyes
4 elongated amber beads for claws
50 cm iron-on vilene
red and blue metallic machine thread

TEMPLATES
cocks (page 160)

▶ Enlarge the design if necessary and prepare the cocks by following the instructions for the *Direct appliqué technique* on page 21. Remember that superimposed pieces do not require underlap seam allowances but where two raw edges meet, one edge must have the underlap allowance included.

▶ Assemble the pieces using a top tracing as a guide, if necessary. Glue the patches in position. Do not use pins as they tend to mark the leather.

▶ Place the assembled cocks onto the jacket and machine straight stitch the entire design, using the machine foot as your seam guide. Leather can be straight stitched because the raw edge will not fray. For a really successful effect be sure to keep your top stitching even.

▶ Attach the rhinestones for eyes and the amber beads for claws.

COCONUT PALMS

This is embroidery with a twentieth century appeal. The palms are created by using traditional embroidery stitches in chunky wools.

MATERIALS
1 loosely woven jumper
1 ball each dark brown, mixed beige and brown, dark green and light green wool
selection of brown wooden beads
iron-on vilene

STITCHES USED
raised chain stitch (page 29)
Pekinese stitch (page 28)
chain stitch (page 28)

TEMPLATE
coconut palms (page 155)

▶ Enlarge the design by following the instructions on page 18.

▶ Place the vilene, *shiny-side down*, over the design and trace over the outlines.

▶ Cut out the palms and iron the vilene directly onto the right side of the jumper.

▶ Using the photograph as a guide, embroider the stems in raised chain stitch, the dark green leaves in Pekinese stitch and the light green leaves in chain stitch.

▶ Stitch the wooden beads in interesting clusters to resemble coconuts.

NOTE If the wools are particularly chunky, six strands of embroidery thread may be used for the base stitches of the raised chain and Pekinese stitches (that is, the basic ladder of the raised chain and the back stitch of the Pekinese).

TROPICAL PARROT

This gay parrot will cheer up any drab top. The touch of beading adds a little glamour for evening wear.

MATERIALS
25 cm each of orange, yellow and blue chintz
small scraps of white and black chintz
matching machine thread
black embroidery thread
black, yellow and crystal seed beads
1 rhinestone

TEMPLATE
parrot (page 155)

▶ Enlarge the design by following the instructions on page 18.

▶ Prepare the design for *Double vilene appliqué* by following the instructions on page 22.

▶ Using matching thread, machine satin stitch all the details. Cut away any excess vilene.

▶ Stitch the rhinestone in position for the eye, crust the upper beak with yellow seed beads and couch the lower beak with black seed beads. Crust a few crystals at the top of the beak.

▶ Hand hem, open zigzag or straight stitch the parrot onto the shirt.

▶ Now couch the black seed beads directly onto the garment to form the claws.

▶ Embroider the branch in chain stitch using three strands of black embroidery thread.

NOTE Always work from the centre, outwards. When machine satin stitching curves, leave the needle in the fabric on the outside of the shape, lift the presser foot and turn. Continue stitching without interrupting the satin stitching.

BRONZE EAGLE

The sensitivity of this design lies in the careful and subtle use of aerosol paint on the fabric.

MATERIALS
1 T-shirt
black and gold thread
selection of bugle and seed beads and
    sequins in blacks, purples and bronze
1 rhinestone for the eye
6 diamond-shaped beads for claws
1 tube black fabric paint
1 can gold aerosol paint
1 can bronze aerosol paint
1 large sheet cardboard

TEMPLATE
eagle (page 168)

▶ Enlarge the design onto the sheet of cardboard by following the instructions on page 18.

▶ Cut out the eagle with sharp pointed scissors, as you would a stencil, and put the eagle aside to use as a reference for the black outlines and beads. Place the cardboard stencil on the garment with the eagle positioned where you would like it.

▶ Secure the cardboard stencil with pins or a few heavy objects.

▶ Spray the eagle first with bronze, concentrating more on the wings than the abdomen. As you spray, be sensitive to the shapes and allow the background to filter through in some areas. Allow a few minutes for drying.

▶ Spray with the gold aerosol, this time concentrating on the abdomen. Do not over-spray as you will lose the bronze tones.

▶ Remove the cardboard stencil when the aerosol paint is quite dry.

▶ Using ball-point fabric paint, paint in the black details. Once dry, the eagle is ready to be beaded.

▶ Use as many exciting beading techniques as you can (see NOTE).

▶ Couch the black section of the beak and attach the rhinestone and diamond-shaped beads.

NOTE On this particular eagle, the eye and claws are crusted with seed beads; three beads are threaded at a time and anchored so that one tiny bead rests on top of two.
The top of the head is beaded with various lengths of dangling bugle beads while the wings are a mixture of different combinations of sequins: for example, sequins alternating with bugle beads, sequins anchored with seed beads, sequins bridged and attached with fine seed beads, and clusters made up of two seed beads, one sequin, three seed beads, one sequin and two seed beads.

PANSIES

A cascade of ten little pansy faces turns an ordinary denim coat into something really special. The flowers lend themselves to embroidery or beading.

STAB or straight stitches, are single, spaced stitches which may be worked evenly, irregularly, long, short or overlapping. The stitches should not be too long or too loose.

MATERIALS
small pieces of yellow, shocking pink, purple, lilac and turquoise glazed cotton
iron-on vilene
small quantity of polyester batting
1 ball chunky green wool
matching machine thread
white, black, yellow, shades of purple, pink and turquoise embroidery thread

STITCHES USED
bullion knots (page 28)
French knots (page 28)
split stitch (see 29)
stab stitch (see Box)
couching (page 29)

TEMPLATE
pansies (page 131)

▶ Trace the pansies directly onto the shiny side of the iron-on vilene. Cut out the shapes and iron them onto the wrong side of the chosen fabric. Cut out the fabric shapes, place them on a larger piece of vilene and machine satin stitch the petal divisions and the outlines in matching thread.

▶ Using the photographs as a guide, embroider the centres of the pansies with black bullion knots and yellow French knots.

▶ Shade the petals with split stitches, stab stitches and bullion knots in various tones of the petal colour.

▶ Once all the pansies have been embroidered, cut away the excess vilene.

▶ Cut a piece of batting the same size as each pansy. Hand hem the pansies and batting onto the coat in a cascade from the front, over the shoulder to the back.

▶ Couch the green wool to form stems and leaves as shown.

▶ For a more glamorous effect, the pansies can also be beaded (see Ribbon handbag on page 46). As a motif, the basic pansy can be used on tablecloths, skirts; Roman blinds, cushions or quilts. Enlarge and reduce the pansies to suit your design.

SILK-MOTH

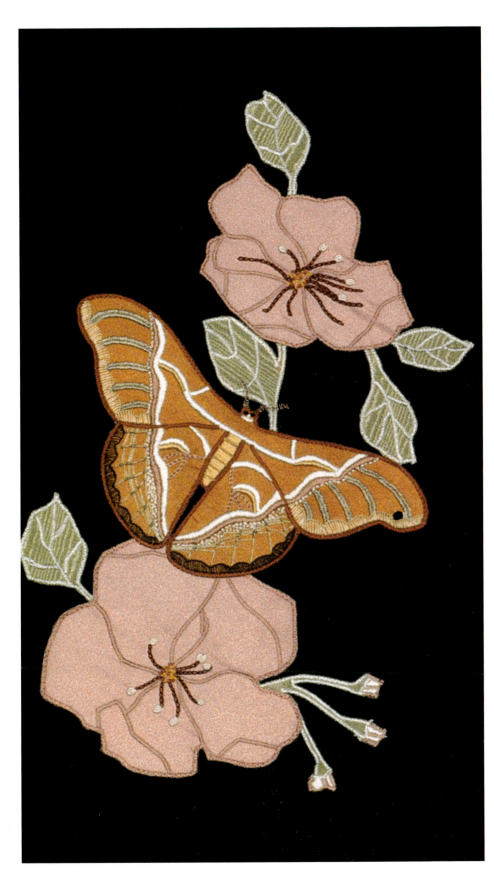

The success of this design lies in embroidering the subtle patterns found in the wings of the tree of heaven silk-moth.

MATERIALS
50 cm bottle green velvet for
   background
25 cm old rose chintz for the flower
25 cm ginger silk for the moth
small scraps green moire taffeta for the
   leaves
iron-on vilene
matching machine thread
black, white, grey, pink, burgundy,
   yellow, brown and beige embroidery
   thread

STITCHES USED
satin stitch (page 29)
French knots (page 28)
buttonhole bars (page 28)
open buttonhole (page 28)
open spider's web (page 28)
chain stitch (page 28)
bullion rosebuds (page 28)

TEMPLATE
flower and silk-moth (page 155)

▶ Enlarge the design, if necessary, by following the instructions on page 18.

▶ Following the instructions for the *Double vilene technique* on page 22, trace, cut and prepare the flowers and moth.

▶ Satin stitch the divisions and outlines in matching thread.

▶ Referring to the photograph, hand embroider the details; use satin stitch, French knots, buttonhole bars, open buttonhole, open spider's web, chain and bullion rosebuds for the silk-moth, and chain, bullion rosebuds and French knots on the flowers.

▶ Cut away the excess vilene.

▶ Prepare the leaves and stems for *Direct appliqué* (page 21) onto the background and satin stitch them into position.

▶ Tack the flowers and silk-moth in position and very carefully open zigzag around each shape.

▶ The design can now be mounted and framed.

PANSIES

A cascade of ten little pansy faces turns an ordinary denim coat into something really special. The flowers lend themselves to embroidery or beading.

STAB or straight stitches, are single, spaced stitches which may be worked evenly, irregularly, long, short or overlapping. The stitches should not be too long or too loose.

MATERIALS
small pieces of yellow, shocking pink, purple, lilac and turquoise glazed cotton
iron-on vilene
small quantity of polyester batting
1 ball chunky green wool
matching machine thread
white, black, yellow, shades of purple, pink and turquoise embroidery thread

STITCHES USED
bullion knots (page 28)
French knots (page 28)
split stitch (see 29)
stab stitch (see Box)
couching (page 29)

TEMPLATE
pansies (page 131)

▶ Trace the pansies directly onto the shiny side of the iron-on vilene. Cut out the shapes and iron them onto the wrong side of the chosen fabric. Cut out the fabric shapes, place them on a larger piece of vilene and machine satin stitch the petal divisions and the outlines in matching thread.

▶ Using the photographs as a guide, embroider the centres of the pansies with black bullion knots and yellow French knots.

▶ Shade the petals with split stitches, stab stitches and bullion knots in various tones of the petal colour.

▶ Once all the pansies have been embroidered, cut away the excess vilene.

▶ Cut a piece of batting the same size as each pansy. Hand hem the pansies and batting onto the coat in a cascade from the front, over the shoulder to the back.

▶ Couch the green wool to form stems and leaves as shown.

▶ For a more glamorous effect, the pansies can also be beaded (see Ribbon handbag on page 46). As a motif, the basic pansy can be used on tablecloths, skirts, Roman blinds, cushions or quilts. Enlarge and reduce the pansies to suit your design.

GIANT EGG

This exciting appliqué was designed by a young art student. It shows the amazing potential of creating art in fabric.

MATERIALS
100 cm x 66 cm piece of calico for the
    background
1 m of calico for the eggshell
polyester stuffing
iron-on vilene
pink, grey and yellow acrylic paints

TEMPLATE
Egg (page 156)

▶ Enlarge the design by following the instructions on page 18 and draw directly onto the calico background with a light pencil.

▶ Referring to the photograph, paint the fabric to create the background and the inside of the broken eggshells.

▶ Now trace the front of the eggshell onto the shiny side of the iron-on vilene.

▶ Cut out the shapes and iron them onto a piece of calico. Cut out this fabric and place the cut-outs onto another piece of calico that is larger than the shapes (see *Double fabric technique* page 23).

▶ Satin stitch around the shapes, leaving a small opening for the stuffing. Insert the stuffing and sew up the opening with satin stitching.

▶ Cut away the excess fabric and hand hem the appliquéd pieces onto the eggshell painting.

▶ Paint the details and shadows onto the three-dimensional shell pieces. The painted appliqué can be stretched onto a frame like an artist's canvas.

STRAWBERRY DELIGHTS

This is a quick and easy appliqué for denim jackets, dinner mats or a patio tablecloth.

MATERIALS
10 cm shocking pink chintz for strawberries
iron-on vilene
small quantity polyester batting
shocking pink and purple machine thread
purple embroidery thread
2 m very narrow green ribbon for bows
2 m each pink and purple fine twisted cord

STITCHES USED
fly stitch (page 29)
blind hem-stitch (page 20)

TEMPLATE
strawberries (page 128)

▶ Trace the required number of strawberries onto iron-on vilene, shiny-side upwards.

▶ Cut out the vilene shapes and iron them onto the wrong side of the fabric. Cut out the fabric shapes and place them onto a larger piece of vilene, shiny side away from the design.

▶ Machine satin stitch around the strawberries in shocking pink thread and then cut away the excess vilene.

▶ Embroider the details in fly stitch using three strands of purple embroidery thread.

▶ Position the strawberries on the jacket (dinner mat or tablecloth), place a small piece of polyester batting under each shape and tack in place.

▶ Arrange the twisted cord connecting the shapes and then couch them using corresponding sheen.

▶ Blind hem-stitch the strawberry appliqués onto the background fabric. Make small bows from the narrow green ribbon and attach them to the top of each strawberry.

TOUCAN TOP

Exotic leather and a few beads make a *stunning evening top. The success of this top is the simplicity of the design and the colour vibration between the garment and the appliquéd toucans.*

MATERIALS
small pieces of black, white and electric
 blue leather
selection of shocking pink, blue and
 black beads (sequins, bugle beads,
 seed beads and rhinestones for eyes)
glue-stick

TEMPLATES
toucans (pages 134-135)

▶ Following the instructions for the *Double vilene technique* on page 22, trace, cut and prepare the toucans. Refer to the photograph and break each bird down into its colour components.

▶ Remember to underlap seam allowances where two raw edges meet.

▶ Assemble the birds on a second piece of vilene using a glue-stick instead of tacking as pins tend to mark the leather.

▶ Machine straight stitch, open zigzag or satin stitch depending on the finish you require. (The leather doesn't fray so it does not have to be satin stitched.)

▶ Use a very sharp needle if the leather is very soft. If the leather is particularly thick, a leather needle will be essential.

▶ Referring to the photograph, bead the birds.

▶ Cut away the excess vilene and hand hem the toucans to a glamorous top.

NOTE Use the same method to make the 'Bird of Paradise' top, but enlarge the design on page 172.

74

TRAPUNTO ROSE

MATERIALS
50 cm cream cotton, polyester-cotton or lawn
50 cm muslin
50 cm calico
40 cm x 40 cm polyester batting
polyester stuffing
cream waxed quilting thread
cream machine thread
apricot, rust, terracotta and cream embroidery thread
4 m x 5 cm wide cream lace
4 m fine cream lace
tiny pearl buttons

STITCHES USED
spider's web (page 28)
short and long extended French knots (page 28)
stem stitch (page 28)
whip stitch (page 20)

TEMPLATE
rose (page 155)

▶ Cut a 40 cm x 40 cm piece of cream background fabric and a corresponding piece of muslin. Tack the muslin to the wrong side of the background fabric.

▶ Enlarge the rose template by following the instructions on page 18. Transfer the design onto the background fabric using an erasable marking pen, dressmaker's pencil or a very light lead pencil.

▶ Make tiny running stitches following the outlines of the trapunto motif using the waxed quilting thread.

▶ When the rose is complete, make small slits in the muslin and insert the stuffing into the cavity of each petal (see *Trapunto quilting* page 39). Close the slits with tiny whip stitches.

▶ Cut another piece of fabric and batting the same size as the background fabric. Sandwich the batting between the top fabrics and the lining and tack the layers together, working from the centre, outwards.

▶ Echo quilt through all the layers using tiny running stitches and following the outlines of the rose at increasing intervals; 5 mm, 10 mm, 20 mm, 25 mm and 50 mm.

▶ Embroider the centre of the rose with a large spider's web, starting with rust, changing to terracotta and then apricot.

▶ Embroider short extended French knots in terracotta and long extended French knots in apricot from the outer edge of the spider's web. Pull firmly through to give the quilted effect.

▶ Stem stitch the leaves with cream embroidery thread.

▶ Cut an 8 cm wide frill, double the circumference of the cushion. Edge the frill with lace and then gather the 5 cm wide lace and the lace-edged fabric frill simultaneously. With right sides together, tack the frill to the quilted top fabric.

▶ Cut two 40 cm x 25 cm pieces of cream fabric for the back.

▶ Turn under 2,5 cm along one long edge of each back piece to form a hem.

▶ Place the backing pieces, right side down, over the top fabric and frill, positioning the hemmed edges in the centre.

▶ Machine straight stitch around the cushion, trim and overlock the seams, clip the curves and turn through.

▶ Sew on tiny pearl buttons and make hand-sewn buttonholes.

▶ Cut two 40 cm x 40 cm pieces of calico for the inner cushion. With right sides together, machine straight stitch around the edges, leaving a small opening. Clip the corners and turn through. Fill with polyester stuffing until plump and then sew up the opening with tiny whip stitches.

This cushion is a fine example of trapunto quilting and embroidery. The coral and apricot embroidery gives definition to the flower, making it more life-like.

MATERIALS

50 cm pure cream cotton
50 cm muslin
50 cm calico for inside cushion
40 cm x 40 cm polyester batting
small packet of polyester stuffing for the
    trapunto areas and the inside cushion
cream waxed quilting thread
matching machine thread
apricot, rust, terracotta and cream
    embroidery thread
1 card cream piped bias binding
tiny pearl buttons

STITCHES USED

running stitch (page 20)
whip stitch (page 20)
French knots (pag 28)
spider's web (page 28)
raised chain stitch (page 29)
fly stitch (page 29)
stab stitch (page 78)
satin stitch (page 29)
Rumanian stitch (page 29)
chain stitch (page 28)
bullion knots (page 28)
buttonhole bars (page 28)

TEMPLATES

shells (pages 138-141)

▶ Cut a 40 cm x 40 cm piece of background fabric and a corresponding piece of muslin. Tack the muslin to the wrong side of the top fabric.

▶ Transfer the shell patterns and mark the quilting pattern on the fabric, using an erasable marking pen, dressmaker's pencil or a very light lead pencil.

▶ Using waxed quilting thread, make tiny running stitches following the outlines of the shells (see *Trapunto* page 39).

▶ Make small slits in the muslin and insert the stuffing into all the cavities. Close the slits with tiny whip stitches.

▶ Cut another piece of fabric and batting the same size as the background fabric and sandwich the batting between the top layers and the lining.

▶ Following the outlines, quilt through all the layers using tiny running stitches. Echo quilt around the shapes at 6 mm intervals.

▶ Decorate the shells with rust, apricot and terracotta embroidery referring to the photograph for ideas. For example, use French knots and spider's web on the star fish; raised chain stitch on the snail shell; fly stitch and stab stitch on the fan shell; satin stitch and Rumanian stitch on the cone-shaped shell and chain stitch and bullions on the cylindrical shell.

▶ To finish off, stitch the piped bias binding to the outer edge of the trapunto top using a zipper foot.

▶ Cut two 40 cm x 25 cm pieces of cream fabric for the back. Turn a hem under along the long edge of each piece. Lap the backs to fit the front and with right sides facing, sew around the cushion.

▶ Clip the curves, overlock the seams and turn through.

▶ Sew on tiny pearl buttons and make hand-sewn buttonholes.

▶ Cut two 40 cm x 40 cm pieces of calico for the inner cushion and machine stitch them together, leaving a small opening. Clip corners and turn through. Fill with polyester stuffing until plump and sew up the opening with whip stitches.

TRAPUNTO SHELLS

These instructions are for a single shell cushion but imagine how beautiful a quilt of different shell blocks would look on a bed that has a view of the ocean beyond.

HARLEQUIN

MATERIALS
80 cm x 70 cm cotton for background
60 cm exciting fabric for harlequin's suit
(patterned for the pastel version with
bows or plain fabric if the suit is to be
beaded)
25 cm white chintz for face, hands and
stockings
small pieces chintz for shoes, skull cap
and cheeks
iron-on vilene
matching machine thread
embroidery thread for face details
3 m gathered white lace
2 m ribbon for bows
1 m ballet ribbon for miniature ballet
shoes
1 pair of miniature satin or porcelain
ballet shoes
selection of sequins, bugle and seed
beads if the suit is to be decorated
a small piece of polyester batting

STITCHES USED
long and short satin stitch (page 29)
satin stitch (page 29)
stab stitch (page 78)

TEMPLATES
harlequin (page 167)

▶ Enlarge the design by following the
instructions on page 18. Trace, cut and
prepare all the shapes, except the face
and cap, for *Direct appliqué* (page 21).

▶ Machine satin stitch the suit, arm,
stockings and shoes in matching thread
onto the background fabric.

▶ Trace, cut and prepare the face and
cap for the *Double vilene technique*
(page 22). Machine satin stitch.

This design combines a number of interesting techniques: embroidery, lace frills, beading and bows. A choice of primary colours and beads will create a high-tech harlequin whereas pastel shades and bows will have a more delicate appeal.

▶ Hand embroider the details on the face using long and short satin stitch for the eyes, satin stitch for the eyelids, eyebrows and mouth and stab stitch for the nose.

▶ Bead the skull cap once the embroidery on the face is complete.

▶ Arrange the layers of lace to form a ruffle on the harlequin suit and hand hem in position.

▶ Cut away the excess vilene and hand hem the face into position, placing a thin piece of batting underneath to give it a slightly raised effect.

▶ Make and attach bows and/or bead the details onto the suit.

▶ Hand hem the ballet ribbon into the hand and tie the miniature ballet shoes onto this ribbon.

POPPY TABLECLOTH

MATERIALS
1,75 m diameter white cotton tablecloth
24 cm wide red cotton for the frill, double the circumference of the tablecloth (about 10 m in length before gathering)
2 m red cotton for bows, ties and poppies
spotted cotton for eight poppies
iron-on vilene
polyester batting
white tape
Velcro
red machine thread
yellow, black and green embroidery thread

STITCHES USED
bullion knots (page 28)
satin stitch (page 29)
stem stitch (page 28)
chain stitch (page 28)

TEMPLATE
poppy (page 130)

▶ Following the instructions for the *Double vilene technique* on page 22, prepare five poppies in plain red and three with superimposed spotted petals alternating with the plain red. Machine satin stitch the poppies in red and cut away the excess vilene.

▶ Referring to the photograph for details, embroider the centre of each poppy with six yellow bullion knots bordered by black bullion knots. Fill in the spaces with green satin stitch using three strands of embroidery thread. Stem stitch the stamens in black, adding a yellow bullion knot to each tip.

▶ Cut the batting out in the shape of each poppy and position the eight poppies on the tablecloth with the batting under each one. Attach the poppies with an open zigzag just inside the satin-stitched edge or hand hem in place.

▶ Draw the curling stems onto the cloth with a dressmaker's pencil. Using three strands of green embroidery thread, embroider the stems in chain stitch.

▶ Fold the frill in half lengthwise and then gather it to fit the tablecloth and stitch in position.

▶ Divide the circumference of the cloth into eight sections and gather the material for a short distance from the frill towards the centre, thus forming a scalloped edge. Secure and strengthen the gathers by stitching a piece of tape behind the gathered sections.

▶ Cut out eight 9 cm x 8 cm rectangles and eight 50 cm x 20 cm rectangles of red cotton for the bows and ties.

▶ Fold the rectangles in half lengthwise, right sides together, and machine stitch along the raw edges leaving a small opening for turning through. Turn through. Wrap a small rectangle around the centre of a large rectangle and hand hem to create a bow tie effect.

▶ Attach a small piece of Velcro to the back of each bow and a corresponding piece to the gathered points on the tablecloth. Attach the bows.

Vibrant red poppies, frill and removable bows make this a gay tablecloth on which to enjoy an alfresco meal. The poppies can also be used most successfully as a quilt design.

WALL HANGING

MATERIALS

86 cm x 61 cm black poplin for
   background
128 cm x 103 cm grey poplin for lining
   and border
25 cm rust, white, grey, beige, mustard,
   brown and dark grey poplin
iron-on vilene
black and grey machine thread
86 cm x 61 cm polyester batting
small brass rings

TEMPLATE

geometric design (page 149)

▶ Enlarge the design by following the
instructions on page 18.

▶ Trace, cut and prepare the shapes for
the *Direct appliqué technique* (page 21).
Add underlap seam allowances where
two raw edges meet.

▶ Tack the entire design onto the
background and machine satin stitch in
black using a wide setting (about 3).
Work from the centre outwards to avoid
puckering.

▶ When all the pieces have been
overlocked, tack the polyester batting to
the back of the patched appliqué.

▶ Quilt the design, using outline stitching,
echo quilting or twin-needle stitching.

▶ Place the lining under the quilted work
and wrap the fabric to the front to form a
10 cm border with a 1 cm turn under.
Machine straight stitch through all the
layers in grey.

▶ Now echo quilt the border with twin-
needle stitching. Hand stitch small brass
rings onto the back of the border for
hanging.

NOTE This pattern can be made using appliqué or patchwork techniques or a combination of the two.
Note that the design is not totally
symmetrical. The Ndebele tribe
draw their designs free-hand, so the
patches are not identical.

The success of this hanging lies in the fine balance of earth colours and black, white and grey. The design has its roots in Ndebele wall paintings. Enlarged, this design would make an exotic quilt.

NDEBELE ARTIST

This appliqué was inspired by a wonderful photograph of an Ndebele artist, busy at work painting the walls of her home in their traditional, geometric patterns. This design incorporates appliqué, wool embroidery and beads.

MATERIALS
50 cm black cotton for background
25 cm each pale and dark blue cotton
small pieces rust-coloured cotton
iron-on vilene
small piece polyester batting
matching machine thread
silver crochet thread for metal bracelets
brown and black embroidery thread for skin and hair
selection of blue, green, red, navy and plum wool for blanket
selection of *non-shiny* (African) pink, blue, red, yellow, black and white seed beads
1 m x 1 cm wide each dark blue and apricot ribbon

STITCHES USED
split stitch (page 29)
French knots (page 28)
weaving (page 29)
couching (page 29)
Pekinese stitch (page 28)
chain stitch (page 28)
raised chain stitch (page 29)
buttonhole bars (page 28)

TEMPLATE
Ndebele artist (page 160)

▶ Enlarge the design by following the instructions on page 18. Trace, cut and prepare the geometric patterns of the walls by following the instructions for *Direct appliqué* (page 21)

▶ Cut out the vilene-backed fabric shapes and machine satin stitch them onto the background fabric.

▶ Open zigzag the blue and apricot ribbon in position.

▶ Trace the figure onto the *non-shiny* side of the iron-on vilene. Iron the cut out shape onto the appliquéd background.

▶ With four strands of brown embroidery thread, split stitch the head and hand. Embroider the hair with French knots using six strands of black embroidery thread.

▶ Embroider the blanket in wools using weaving, couching, Pekinese, chain stitch filled with French knots, and raised chain. Use the photograph as your guide.

▶ Using silver crochet thread, embroider buttonhole bars to form the metal bracelets.

▶ Couch the beads onto the head in horizontal lanes. Thread the beads onto a double thread to resemble a long necklace, and then secure the beads to the head with a small anchoring stitch between every second bead.

▶ For the raised beading on the necklaces, couch the beads in short vertical lanes over a piece of polyester batting.

▶ For the arm bracelets, embroider a layer of chain stitches in fine wool beneath the beads to give a slightly raised effect (must not be as high as the necklaces with the wadding beneath the beads).

▶ The finished design can be quilted and lined and used as a soft wall hanging or it can be framed.

NDEBELE DRESS

This particular patchwork was inspired by the designs on the African houses of the Ndebele tribe. Its success relies on the vibrant colours on a strong navy African print background.

MATERIALS
50 cm red cotton
small scrap turquoise-green cotton
1 card each red, white, turquoise, purple, and yellow bias binding
matching machine thread

TEMPLATES
yoke design (page 124)
border designs (pages 124-126)

For the skirt border
▶ Cut a 167 cm x 13 cm strip of red fabric. (If the skirt is very full, increase the longer measurement to suit the hem measurement of your garment.) Cut four triangles of turquoise-green fabric and four triangles of red for the pyramid shapes (Sketch A).

▶ Position the turquoise-green and then the red triangle on the red border strip and open zigzag in place. Using Sketches A, B and C and the photograph as a guide, place the bias binding strips on the background and machine straight stitch or open zigzag in matching thread. For a small dress, use the pyramid twice, separating the front (stepped) design from the back (scissors) design. For larger dresses, repeat the three basic designs as many times as required.

▶ Do not incorporate the turquoise outer bias binding until the red strip is attached to the skirt.

▶ Place the red border on the skirt and machine zigzag in place. Finish off the edge of the red border with the turquoise bias binding.

For the yoke
▶ Using Sketch D and referring to the photograph, cut one triangle out of the turquoise-green fabric and attach it directly to the yoke with open zigzag.

▶ Machine the bias binding directly onto the yoke using the same technique as the skirt border.

> **NOTE** This set of instructions is suitable for a dress for a three or four year old. For larger or smaller dresses, simply repeat or omit some of the border designs.

BEACH PALS

The inspiration for this design was a delightful greetings card. There is a fine balance of hand and machine work and the background hues are achieved by spraying the fabric with aerosol paint.

FEATHER STITCH Begin with a single feather stitch. The base of the first stitch forms the branch of the second stitch. Make a stitch to the left on the same level and then to the right Continue working these two movements alternately.

MATERIALS
1 m x 30 cm pale grey linen
1 m x 30 cm mid-blue linen
1 m x 40 cm apricot linen
1 m x 10 cm navy linen
23 cm brown and white pinstripe for shirt
scraps of white cotton for collar and cuffs
20 cm denim for jeans
25 cm cream cotton for faces, hands and legs
25 cm yellow cotton for hair
small piece of brown felt for dog
scrap of spotted red cotton for hankie and dog's collar
25 cm of blue sprigged cotton for dress
30 cm white anglaise fabric for apron
25 cm fine cross-stitch fabric for hat
iron-on vilene
little batting
blue, white, brown, yellow, cream and red embroidery thread
2 m x 2 cm wide white ribbon
2 m x 1 cm wide white ribbon
1 m x 3 mm wide white ribbon
3 m white anglaise lace for apron and hat
tiny white pearl buttons for apron
white, pink, grey and blue aerosol paint
gut

STITCHES USED
spider's web (page 28)
fly stitch (page 29)
satin stitch (page 29)
raised chain stitch (page 29)
detached chain stitch (page 28)
feather stitch (see Box)
grub roses (page 28)
French knots (page 28)
buttonhole stitch (page 28)
bullion rosebuds (page 28)

TEMPLATE
beach scene (page 159)

▶ Using the photograph as a guide, spray the four linen fabrics with white, pink, grey and blue aerosol paint. Try to create the illusion of shadows on the beach, movement in the waves and wispy clouds in the sky.

▶ Enlarge the design by following the instructions on page 18.

▶ When the paint is dry, prepare the vilene pieces for the background using the *Direct appliqué technique* (page 21). Iron the vilene onto the linen background fabrics and machine satin stitch them together to form one piece of background.

▶ Prepare the figures, dog and the hat for the *Double vilene technique* (page 22).

▶ Make the boy's hankie by following the instructions for the *Double fabric technique* on page 23. The hankie will be double-sided and will hang free.

▶ Make the girl's arm in the same way so that the hat can be placed under the hand.

▶ Position the anglaise lace just under the edge of the apron and tack.

▶ Machine satin stitch all the details on the figures.

▶ Once all the machining is complete, hand embroider a row of white spider's web daisies, joined with feather stitch, along the bottom of the apron. Finish off by attaching a tiny pearl to the centre of each daisy.

▶ Embroider the boy's eye in blue satin stitch and add a few gut eyelashes. Using a double strand of gut, begin on the right side of the work, leaving the two strands protruding approximately 1 cm. Make a back stitch and exit again on the right side of the work. Cut off, leaving the gut protruding by 1 cm. Continue in this way until enough eyelashes have been made.

▶ Embroider grub roses, French knot forget-me-nots, spider's web daisies or any other flowers that take your fancy on the hat brim.

▶ French knot the waves and satin stitch the sea gulls, using three strands of white embroidery thread. Use buttonhole stitch on the under-wings to give the wings definition.

▶ Cut away the excess vilene around the figures and the dog and attach them to the background fabric using straight stitch just inside the overlocked edge.

▶ To complete the hat, stitch the anglaise lace to the rim. Run a gathering thread through the 1 cm wide white ribbon and pull it up firmly. Hem-stitch this gathered ribbon to the crown of the hat and make a small bow from the 3 mm wide ribbon. Attach this little bow next to the flowers.

▶ Place a small piece of stuffing under the crown of the hat and hem-stitch the hat in position under the girl's arm.

▶ Embroider the fishing rod in raised chain stitch using three strands of brown embroidery thread. Using ginger-brown thread, embroider the fishing line in single chain stitch.

▶ Pleat the 2 cm wide ribbon and attach it to the back of the apron with a couple of bullion rosebuds. Anchor the lengths of ribbon with feather (or fly) stitch.

LET'S GO SAILING

MATERIALS
25 cm each of four shades of blue chintz
 for the clouds
50 cm cotton moire design fabric for
 water
25 cm red, blue and cream cotton for
 lighthouse
25 cm beige chintz for quayside
25 cm red, aquamarine, light and dark
 yellow cotton for yachts
iron-on vilene
matching machine thread
embroidery thread in various colours for
 flowers on bank
3 m white soutache (cord) for rigging

STITCHES USED
French knots (page 28)
chain stitch (page 28)
bullion knots (page 28)
buttonhole stitch (page 28)

TEMPLATE
seaside scene (page 157)

▶ Enlarge the design by following the
instructions on page 18.

▶ Prepare the vilene and fabric pieces
for the clouds, lighthouse, quayside and
water using the *Direct appliqué
technique* on page 21.

▶ Pin, baste and machine satin stitch the
shapes together to form the background,
referring to the photograph for machine
thread choice. Do not forget to add
underlap seam allowances.

▶ Prepare the yachts for the *Double
vilene technique* by following the
instructions on page 22.

▶ Machine satin stitch the yachts and
trim away the excess vilene. Embroider
the details on the sails using back or stem
stitch.

▶ Embroider the heads of the four figures
with French knots to create the hair.

▶ Position the yachts and open zigzag
them onto the background, attaching
the rigging cord at the same time.

▶ Embroider a few waves in blue chain
stitch.

▶ Embellish the bank with gay flowers
such as white French knot daisies, red
bullion rosebuds, blue bullion delphiniums and buttonhole black-eyed Susans.

Dominant primary colours and a wonderful design make this appliqué a must for a boy's room or seaside cottage. It combines machine and hand work and both Direct appliqué and the Double vilene technique are used.

The movement in this design is created by a change in the scale of the sails, the diagonal stripes and the suggestion of waves lapping against the sails.

The composition is particularly good – the strong verticals are balanced by horizontal sand dunes, with the sails forming a series of triangles within triangles.

MATERIALS

1 m printed fabric suitable for water and
  sand
25 cm each of blue, orange, shocking
  pink, white, turquoise and apple green
  cotton for sails
1,5 m polyester batting
iron-on vilene
1 m cream calico for lining and border
matching machine thread
selection of brightly coloured
  embroidery threads for numbers and
  stripes on the sails
grey, white and blue pearl embroidery
  thread for the waves
4 m white cotton twist cord

STITCHES USED

French knots (page 28)
satin stitch (page 29)
long and short satin stitch (page 29)
raised chain stitch (page 29)
spider's web (page 28)

TEMPLATE

windsurfers (page 158)

▶ Enlarge the design by following the instructions on page 18.

▶ Following the instructions for the *Double vilene technique* on page 22, trace, cut and prepare the sails. Machine stitch all the stripes on the sails first and then overlock the outlines in matching machine thread. Make a selection of different sized sails.

▶ Embroider the logos on the sails in spider's web and the numbers in long and short satin stitch. Embroider the stripes on the small sails in raised chain.

▶ The background fabric used in the photograph was purchased pre-printed with water and dunes. If suitable fabric is not available, cut interesting shapes in blue, cream and grey and satin stitch them together to form the background.

▶ Attach the polyester batting to the background by tacking along the diagonals.

▶ Top stitch the grey and blue areas with twin-needle stitching and then echo quilt the cream sand dunes.

▶ Cut pieces of batting the same size as each sail and hand hem or open zigzag the sails in position with the batting sandwiched in between.

▶ Embroider crests of waves in grey, blue and white French knots.

▶ Cut a piece of cream calico that is 16 cm larger all round than the appliqué for the lining and border.

▶ The finished border is 7,5 cm wide with a 1 cm turn under. If a well-rounded border is required, add another strip of polyester batting into the roll.

▶ Beginning at the bottom right hand corner, hand hem the border to the appliqué, attaching the white cord at the same time. Knot the two ends of cord together in the bottom right hand corner and attach small brass rings to the back of the border for hanging.

WIND SURFING

What a fun way to display those special badges!

MATERIALS for Hermes
63 cm cream cotton for background
50 cm black cotton for the circle
50 cm bright yellow cotton for figure
matching machine thread
yellow and black embroidery thread
selection of badges

STITCHES USED
Rumanian stitch (page 28)
chain stitch (page 28)
raised chain stitch (page 29)

TEMPLATE
Hermes (page 153)

▶ Enlarge the design by following the instructions on page 18. Cut a 50 cm diameter circle out of the black cotton.

▶ Trace, cut out and prepare the Hermes figure for *Direct appliqué* (page 21) onto the black circle. Machine satin stitch the figure in position.

▶ Machine satin stitch the words with a width setting of 3.

▶ Draw the laurel leaves and other details onto the fabric and embroider with Rumanian, chain and raised chain stitches.

▶ Centre the black circle on the background fabric and tack in position. Stay stitch with an open zigzag to prevent puckering and then overlock.

▶ Hand hem the badges in place and embroider special times and dates for that personal touch.

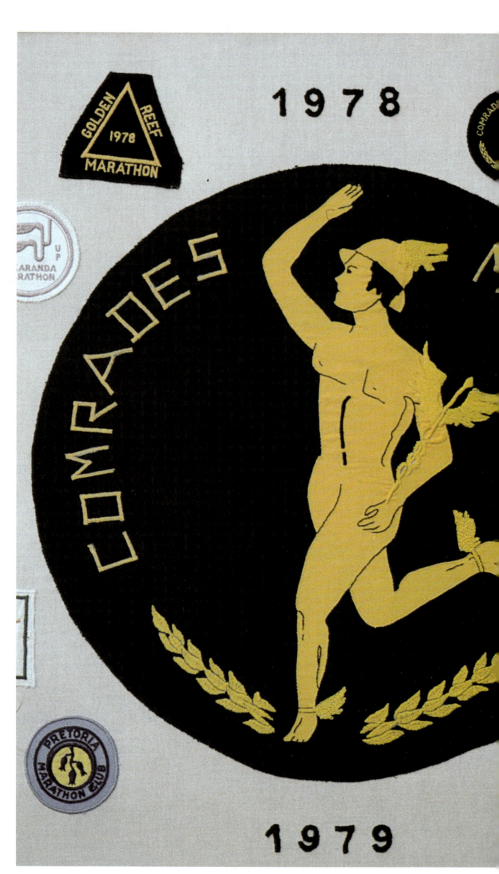

MATERIALS for marathon runner
The materials required for this runner are highly personal. Here we have used the actual vest and running shorts of this particular jogger's club. His personal number, scarf and hankie are made using the *Double fabric technique* (page 23) so they can be twisted or pinned to look authentic. The shoes are suede, socks are towelling and the pith helmet is linen and leather.

50 cm black chintz for silhouette
75 cm cream linen for background
matching machine thread
a selection of embroidery threads

TEMPLATE
single runner (page 153)

▶ Find a photograph of the jogger in a victory pose. Enlarge the figure as a silhouette. Use the photograph as a guide and create the same personal touches using the colours and gear of the jogger being portrayed.

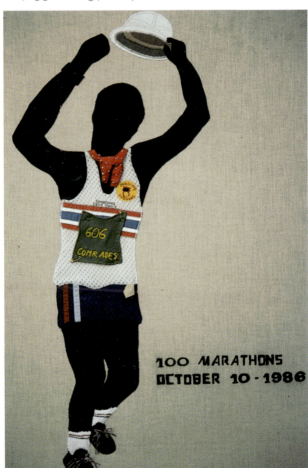

Geometric shapes in various textures can be appliquéd or patched to create this city. The neutrality of the ancient buildings is broken by the modern touches of TV aerials and street lamps. This design can be adapted to resemble any old Mediterranean village if the gold dome is omitted.

MATERIALS
105 cm x 80 cm pale grey cotton for background
50 cm or 25 cm each of raw silk, linen, hessian, wool, corduroy and moire taffeta depending on choice of building and fabric
25 cm gold lamé for the dome
iron-on vilene (if design is appliquéd)
small pieces of gingham for window insets
matching machine thread
gold metallic embroidery thread
interesting coloured embroidery threads for washing on line

STITCHES USED
satin stitch (page 29)
chain stitch (page 28)
split stitch (page 29)
any woven stitches (page 28-29)
weaving (page 29)

TEMPLATE
buildings (page 163)

▶ Enlarge the design by following the instructions on page 18.

For patching or hand appliqué
▶ If the design is to be patched or hand appliquéd, make templates of all the buildings and cut out the fabric with a 6 mm seam allowance all round.

▶ Whip the buildings together and then hand hem the outline to the skyline.

For machine appliqué
▶ Work from the back sky forwards and attach the buildings in position using the *Direct appliqué technique* (page 21). Remember to underlap seam allowances where two raw edges will meet.

▶ The windows, canopies and domes are superimposed and do not require extra seam allowances.

▶ Use twin-needle stitching to create the illusion of bricks and roof tops.

▶ Hand embroider the street lamps in gold satin stitch and the TV aerials in black and gold chain stitch.

▶ Using interesting colours, embroider cloths and a shirt onto a washing line. Use split stitch or continuous chain for the shirt and weaving, Pekinese and raised chain stitch for the cloths.

COUNTRY KITCHEN

This design combines appliqué patchwork and embroidery.

MATERIALS
50 cm red gingham for wallpaper
50 cm cream linen for floor
25 cm black cotton for coal stove
25 cm anglaise for granny's apron
25 cm black granny print fabric for dress
25 cm grey cotton
small scraps brightly coloured cotton for patchwork tablecloth, cake, cat, tin, clock, vase, rolling pin and basket
iron-on vilene
matching machine thread
grey, black, blue, red and yellow embroidery thread
gold metallic thread for spectacles
small pieces of braid and lace for shelf

STITCHES USED
satin stitch (page 29)
chain stitch (page 28)
bullion rosebuds (page 28)
spider's web (page 28)
French knots (page 28)
back stitch (page 28)
bullion knots (page 28)

TEMPLATE
country kitchen (page 142)

*NOTE If patchwork-patterned material is used, prepare the tablecloth using the *Direct appliqué technique* (page 21).

▶ Enlarge the design by following the instructions on page 18.

▶ With right sides together, machine straight stitch the gingham and linen together to form a background.

▶ Following the instructions for *Direct appliqué*, trace, cut and prepare the pieces for the stove. Tack and machine satin stitch the stove pieces to the background. For delineation on the stove, stitch in grey thread.

▶ Following the instructions for the *Double vilene technique* on page 22, trace, cut and prepare the granny. Machine satin stitch all the pieces in matching colours.

▶ Using the looping foot on your machine, make rows of loops and a circular bun-shape to form the granny's hair.

▶ Hand embroider the granny's eyes in black, blue and white satin stitch and her spectacles in gold chain stitch.

▶ Cut away the excess vilene, position the figure on the background and open zigzag in place.

▶ Make all the small objects using the *Double vilene technique* and then machine stitch or hand hem them in place.

▶ Make the patchwork tablecloth using a 2 cm square template or material that is printed to look like patchwork*.

▶ Machine satin stitch the table onto the background. Add the cake, tin and rolling pin.

▶ Embroider the cherries on the cake in red bullion rosebuds; the cookies in brown spider's webs and the salt and pepper in French knots. Satin stitch the daisies in the vase; back stitch the numbers on the clock and bullion knot the nails in the floor boards. Satin stitch the eyes and nose of the cat in white and black.

▶ Open zigzag the braid and lace in position for a shelf.

TEA FOR TWO

MATERIALS
66 cm black and white spotted taffeta
    for background
25 cm black and grey satin for the
    tablecloth
50 cm pink and silver satin for the sofa
36 cm each of burgundy and blue
    striped silks
25 cm plum suede for the hats and
    gloves
25 cm black and beige chintz for the
    hair
25 cm cream cotton for the faces and
    arms
25 cm black suede for the handbags
25 cm plain burgundy silk for the
    waistcoat
iron-on vilene
matching machine thread
embroidery thread for the face details
selection of buckles, buttons, chains
1 m x 2,5 cm wide pink ribbon
1 m x 3 mm wide plum ribbon
a little rouge

STITCHES USED
satin stitch (page 29)
back stitch (page 28)
long and short satin stitch (page 29)
stem stitch (page 28)
French knots (page 28)

TEMPLATE
ladies (page 162)

The inspiration for this delightful appliqué was a charming greetings card. Great fun can be had playing with the buttons, bows, buckles, silks and satins.

▶ Enlarge the design by following the instructions on page 18.

▶ Prepare the background, sofa and tablecloth for *Direct appliqué* (page 21). Satin stitch these pieces together.

▶ Following the instructions for the *Double vilene technique* on page 22, trace, cut and prepare the figures.

▶ Change the direction of the striped silk of the auburn-haired figure to give the effect of a waistcoat. Machine satin stitch the figures in matching thread.

▶ Using the looping foot on your machine, make the hair using matching thread.

▶ Using two strands of embroidery thread, hand embroider all the facial details. Use satin stitch for the eyelids and mouth; back stitch for eye line, nose and brow; long and short satin stitch for eyes; stem stitch for lower eye and a French knot for each pupil.

▶ Make the bows on the hats and stitch all the trimmings onto the blouses and bags.

▶ Cut away the excess vilene and machine straight stitch or open zigzag the figures into position at the table.

▶ Lightly hand paint the cheeks with rouge. .

WHEAT FIELDS

MATERIALS
58 cm cream cotton or linen for
 foreground
25 cm blue/grey linen for sky
25 cm each plain green, sprigged and
 wheat-coloured cottons
small scraps subdued plain and
 patterned cottons for peasants clothes
 and the little houses
iron-on vilene
matching machine thread
black, cream and a selection of yellow
 and beige embroidery thread

STITCHES USED
Pekinese stitch (page 29)
raised chain stitch (page 29)
chain stitch (page 28)
bullion knots (page 28)
French knots (page 28)

TEMPLATE
wheat fields (page 154)

▶ Enlarge the design by following the
instructions on page 18. Trace, cut and
prepare the fields, hills, bushes and sky
for the *Direct appliqué technique*
(page 21).

▶ Satin stitch the shapes with matching
thread to make one large working
background.

▶ Now experiment with different cams
and settings. Follow the direction lines as
you work the foreground fields.

▶ Following the instructions for the *Double
vilene technique* on page 22, trace, cut
and prepare the figures and houses.

▶ Machine satin stitch in matching
colours and then cut away the excess
vilene.

▶ Use the looping foot (page 33) to
create the hair and some of the distant
fields.

▶ Open zigzag the figures and houses
into position.

▶ Hand embroider the distant haystacks
in Pekinese; the sheaves of wheat in
raised chain stitch and the ears of wheat
in chain and bullion knots.

▶ Hand embroider the windows and
sickle in satin stitch and the man's beard
in French knots using black thread.

This design provides ample opportunity for experimentation with machine effects using different cams (discs) and settings.

COSMOS

MATERIALS
small pieces of white, pink and lilac
 cotton, chintz, satin or silk*
iron-on vilene
shades of pink and lilac machine thread
green, yellow and shades of pink
 embroidery thread

STITCHES USED
French knots (page 28)
extended French knots (page 28)
stem stitch (page 28)

TEMPLATE
cosmos (page 154)

▸ Enlarge the design by following the
instructions on page 18.

▸ Trace the design directly onto the shiny
side of the vilene. Cut out the vilene
shapes and iron them onto the wrong
side of the fabric.

▸ If the flowers are to be appliquéd onto
small items, such as cushions, use the
Direct appliqué technique (page 21). For
garments, or large creations such as
cloths, quilts or wall hangings, use the
Double vilene technique (page 22).

▸ Machine satin stitch the details on the
flowers, then hand embroider the centres
using French knots and extended French
knots. Hand embroider the leaves and
stems in stem stitch.

*NOTE The amount of fabric will depend on how many flowers are required for your design.

Rene + Ulli

In nature these wild daisies are shades
of pink, lilac, burgundy and white.
They lend themselves to appliqué on
garments, tablecloths, blinds and
cushions. The design could be
enlarged and appliquéd onto a quilt
which would resemble a field of wild
flowers.

MATERIALS

1,5 m pure cotton
25 cm each of various shades of green, pink, plum, lilac, purple, blue, orange, yellow and white chintz
scraps of moire taffeta and organza
scraps of net for butterflies, spider and dragonfly
iron-on vilene
matching machine thread
selection of embroidery threads
crystal beads
polyester stuffing

STITCHES USED

satin stitch (page 29)
spider's web (page 28)
French knots (page 28)
bullion knots (page 28)
chain stitch (page 28)
back stitch (page 28)
raised chain stitch (page 29)
stem stitch (page 28)

This is a very large picture made up of a pot pourri of beautiful flowers and interesting insects. All the flowers are made using the Double vilene technique and then hand embroidered and assembled on a cream, pure cotton background.

▶ Enlarge all the flower designs by following the instructions on page 18 and trace them onto the shiny side of iron-on vilene. Cut out the designs and iron them, *shiny-side down,* onto the relevant fabrics as follows:

dog roses in pale pink
irises in deep purple and blue
cosmos in pinks, plum and white
arum lilies in pale and bright yellow
frangipani in pale yellow
freesias in shocking pink, orange and
   lilac
blossoms in white
foxgloves in pink and plum
leaves in various shades of green

▶ Following the *Double vilene technique* described on page 22, position the flowers and leaves on another piece of vilene and machine satin stitch around each design. Cut out the designs without cutting into the stitching.

▶ Embroider the details on the flowers with spider's webs, French knots, bullion knots and satin stitch.

▶ Blind hem-stitch the flowers in position on the background fabric.

▶ Trace the insects onto the shiny side of the iron-on vilene and cut them out. Place them, *shiny-side down,* onto the relevant fabrics, iron them on and cut them out.

▶ Following the *Double fabric technique* on page 23, machine satin stitch the insects (butterflies and dragonfly) onto a second piece of fabric, and not vilene, so that they can be attached by the abdomen only and the wings stand free. Machine satin stitch, then cut out the shapes.

▶ Embroider the patterns on the butterflies using any of the embroidery stitches illustrated on pages 28-29 (use the photograph as your guide to stitch choice.)

▶ Trace, cut and prepare the spider using the *Double vilene technique* described on page 22. Embroider the abdomen in raised chain and French knots. Prepare the spider's legs using the *Double fabric technique* on page 23 and leave a small edge which can be frayed to give the 'hairy' effect.

▶ Embroider the web using silver metallic thread and chain stitch, adding a few crystal seed beads onto the chain to suggest dewdrops.

▶ Place a small piece of stuffing under the spider's abdomen and slip stitch it onto the web.

▶ Embroider the stems using stem stitch, back stitch, chain and/or raised chain stitch. Add a caterpillar using bullion knots, and striped humming bees using satin stitch for the abdomens, bullion rosebuds for the heads and split stitch for the wings.

TEMPLATES

MATERIALS

1 m cream cotton or raw silk for
  background
50 cm dark cream chintz for house walls
25 cm textured brown fabric for roof
25 cm rust hessian for path
25 cm bottle-green cotton for
  foreground
25 cm each brown, green and white
  fabric for trees and birds
small scraps brown, rust and granny print
  fabric for windows
brown wool for door
25 cm pale green fabric for tree
small pieces orange and yellow cotton
  for nasturtiums; blue cotton for daisies;
  white and green chintz for lilies and
  leaves
1,25 m cream cotton for lining and
  border
iron-on vilene
matching machine thread
selection brightly coloured embroidery
  threads
50 cm lace for curtains
1 m polyester batting
polyester stuffing

STITCHES USED

variety of stitches (pages 28-29)

TEMPLATE

English country garden (pages 150-151)

▶ Enlarge the design by following the
instructions on page 18.

▶ Trace, cut and prepare the pieces of
the house for the *Double vilene
technique* as described on page 22.

▶ Assemble and machine satin stitch in
matching machine thread, inserting the
cream lace curtains as you do so.

▶ Top stitch the front door with twin-
needle stitching (page 40).

▶ Cut away the excess vilene and open
zigzag the house onto the background
fabric.

▶ Trace, cut and assemble the path, the
trees and the dark green area directly
onto the background (see *Direct
appliqué*, page 21) and satin stitch in
place.

▶ Trace, cut and prepare the birds,
waterlilies and nasturtiums using the
Double vilene technique on page 22.

▶ Decorate the flower centres with bullion
knots, French knots and extended French
knots. Cut away the excess vilene and
then hand hem them onto the
background fabric.

▶ Transfer the rest of the flowers and
insects onto the fabric using one of the
methods described on page 18.
Embroider them in bold colours using the
basic stitches on pages 28-29.

▶ Tack the batting to the appliquéd
fabric and hand quilt along all the fabric
outlines using tiny running stitches and
two strands of cream embroidery or
quilting thread.

▶ Using a waxed quilting thread or four
strands of cream embroidery thread,
French knot the cream background in an
interesting pattern.

▶ Cut the lining and border 25 cm larger
all round than the appliqué. Roll the
border to meet the appliqué, adding
more stuffing if a larger roll is required.
Hand hem the border and decorate it
with the embroidery of your choice using
cream embroidery thread.

ENGLISH COUNTRY GARDEN

This design makes full use of appliqué and embroidery. The multi-coloured flowers grow in profusion around the fairy tale house.

TUDOR HOUSE

▶ Enlarge the design by following the instructions on page 18. Following the instructions for *Direct Appliqué* on page 21, prepare and machine satin stitch the house, path, lawn, fence and bushes onto the background fabric.

▶ Twin-needle the dormer roof by following the instructions on page 40.

▶ Embroider the house windows using laid-work, and couch and knot the soutache in place to form the front door (see page 34).

▶ Cut the fabric for the girls' dresses slightly larger than the original drawings. Do not use vilene. Gather and shape the fabric as you hand hem the pieces in place. Small amounts of stuffing can be inserted to help with contouring.

▶ Cut out circles of pink stocking for the hands and faces and fill them with stuffing. Run a gathering thread around the circles and pull up to form a ball-shape. Contour each face with tiny French knot eyes and stab stitch nose and mouth. Shape the faces as you hem them in place on the background. For the hands, pull up a stuffed circle of pink stocking and suggest finger divisions with single stitches, contouring at the same time.

▶ Satin stitch the hair on the crown and make a long plait on the one figure using six strands of embroidery thread.

▶ Make silk ringlets on the other figure by pulling off the coils from a silk gown cord. Catch the coils in position around the little face.

▶ Embroider flowers on the hat and in her hands using grub roses, forget-me-nots (French knots), daisies (spider's web) and leaves (Rumanian).

▶ Weave a little basket with very narrow ribbons. Make vertical strips in parallel lanes in one colour by hand hemming the top and base of each strip in position. Weave a ribbon in a contrasting colour over and under these strips.

▶ Embroider the shoes with raised chain stitch and the socks with Rumanian stitch. Make bullion knots in pairs on the shoes, thread very narrow red ribbon under the bullions and tie the ribbon as you would shoe laces.

MATERIALS

122 cm x 86 cm beige cotton for background
50 cm beige linen for house walls
25 cm dark beige linen for roof
25 cm medium brown wool fabric for wooden beams and path
25 cm dark brown wool fabric for fence
25 cm light green cotton for lawn and bushes
25 cm each tiny sprigged fabric for dresses
small pieces of apricot linen for stepping stones, hats and window frames
pink stockings for faces and hands
silk flowers
iron-on vilene
matching machine thread
selection of embroidery threads
small pieces of ochre and brown soutache for the front door
scraps of lace and ribbon for basket and bows
polyester stuffing
rust-coloured silk gown cord for hair

STITCHES USED

grub roses (page 28)
laid-work (page 29)
French knots (page 28)
stab stitch (page 78)
satin stitch (page 29)
spider's web (page 28)
Rumanian stitch (page 29)
bullion knots (page 28)
Pekinese stitch (page 28)
detached chain stitch (page 29)
extended French knots (page 28)
buttonhole stitch (page 28)

TEMPLATES

house (page 148)
girls (pages 146-147)

▶ Embroider the flowers in the garden using the basic embroidery stitches on pages 28 and 29 and silk flowers (page 34). Choose your own colour and flower combinations, for example grub roses, bullion knot rosebuds, French knot forget-me-nots, bullion delphiniums, Pekinese creepers, spider's web daisies, detached chain daisies and extended French knot grass.

▶ Use bullion knots, spider's web, French knots, extended French knots and

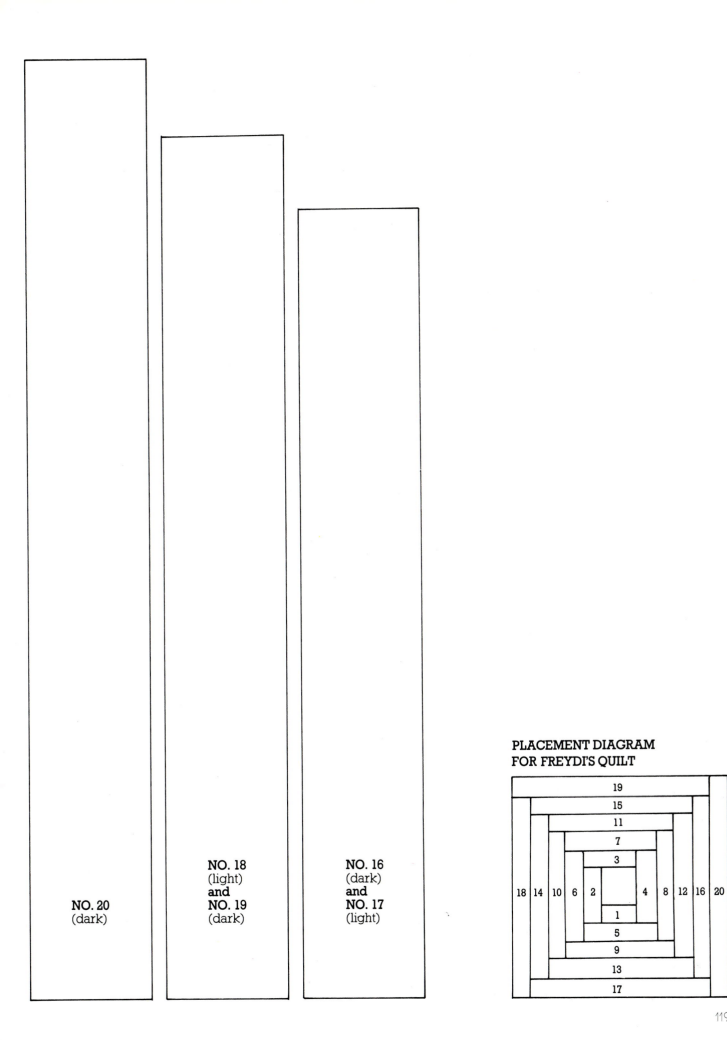

NO. 20
(dark)

NO. 18
(light)
and
NO. 19
(dark)

NO. 16
(dark)
and
NO. 17
(light)

PLACEMENT DIAGRAM
FOR FREYDI'S QUILT

					19					
					15					
					11					
					7					
					3					
18	14	10	6	2		4	8	12	16	20
					1					
					5					
					9					
					13					
					17					

119

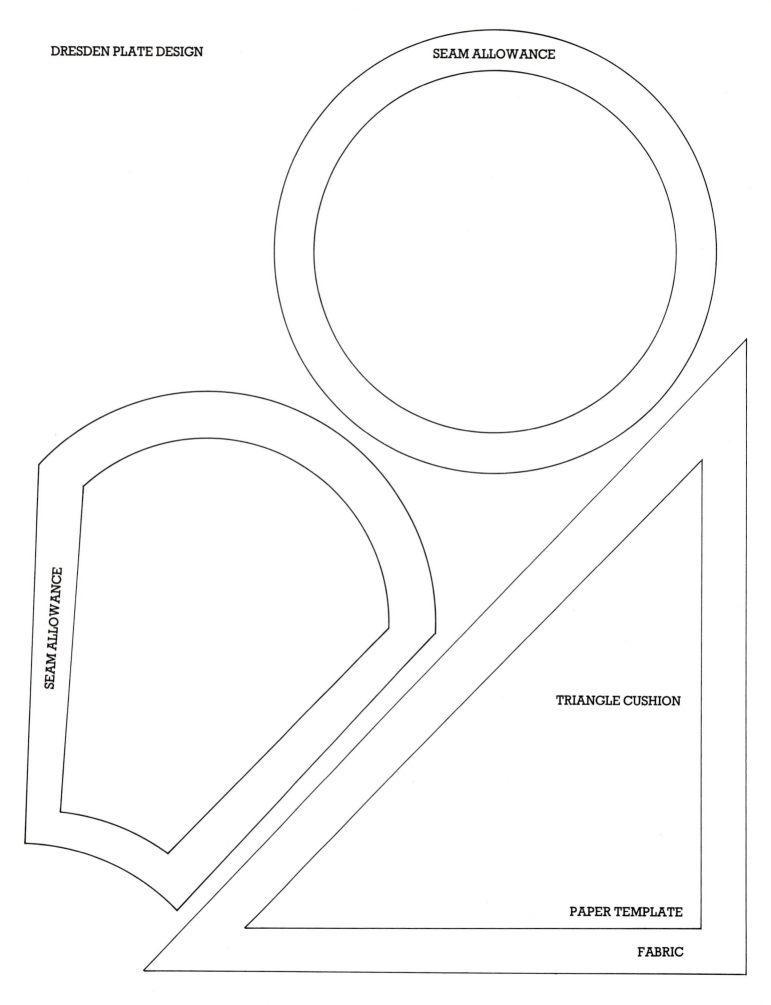

DRESDEN PLATE DESIGN

SEAM ALLOWANCE

SEAM ALLOWANCE

TRIANGLE CUSHION

PAPER TEMPLATE

FABRIC

EIGHT POINT STAR

A

B

C

1

2

121

122

JACOB'S LADDER

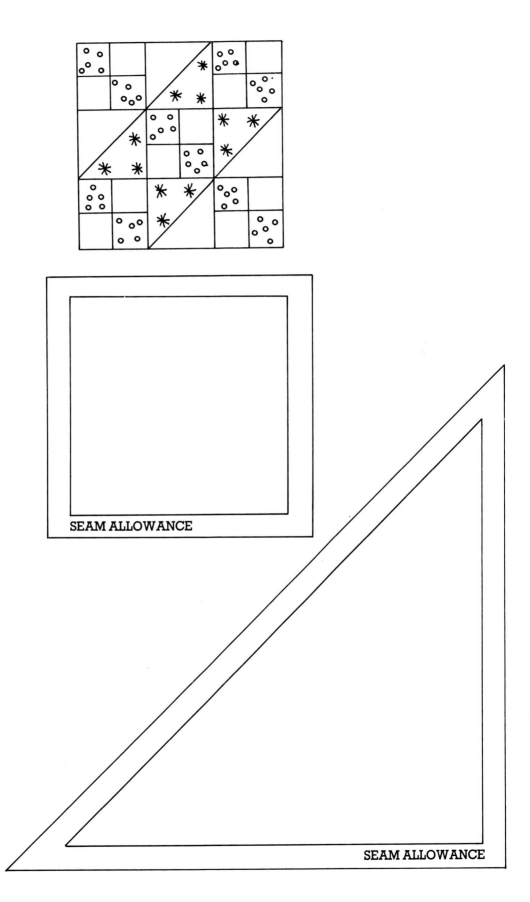

SEAM ALLOWANCE

SEAM ALLOWANCE

NDEBELE DRESS

SKETCH D   YOKE DESIGN

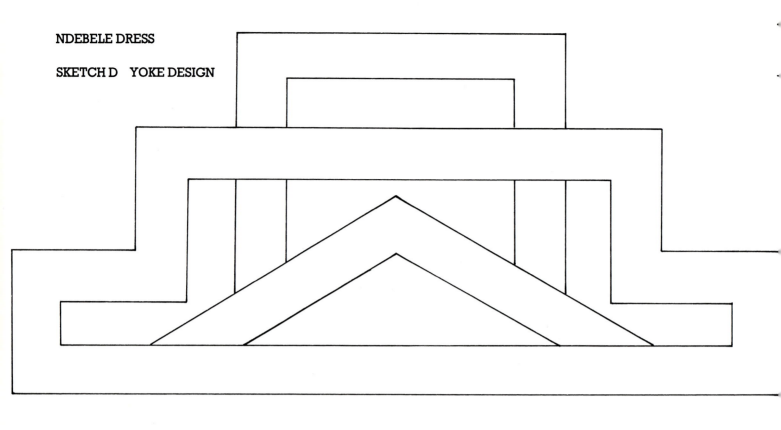

SKETCH B   STEP DESIGN

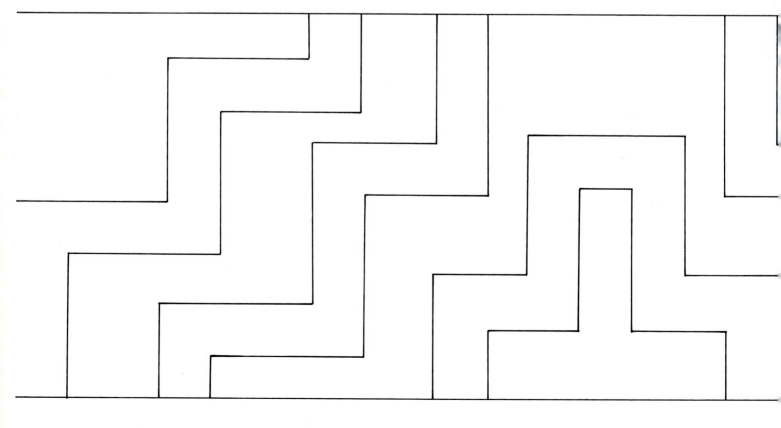

SKETCH A   PYRAMID DESIGN

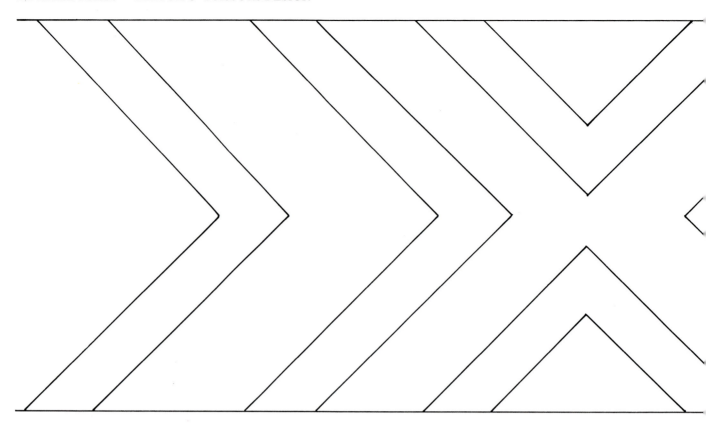

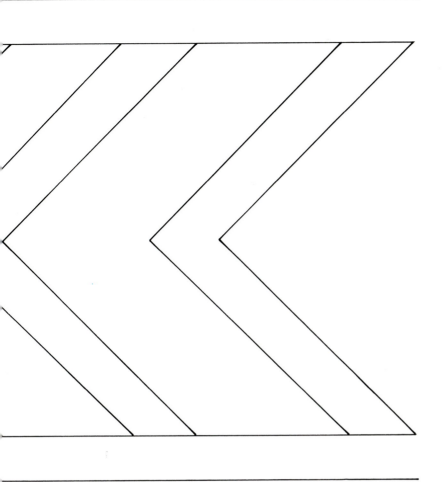

POPPY

PANSIES

LOVEBIRDS (finished size of Birds of a Feather 61 cm x 51 cm)

TOUCAN

TOUCAN

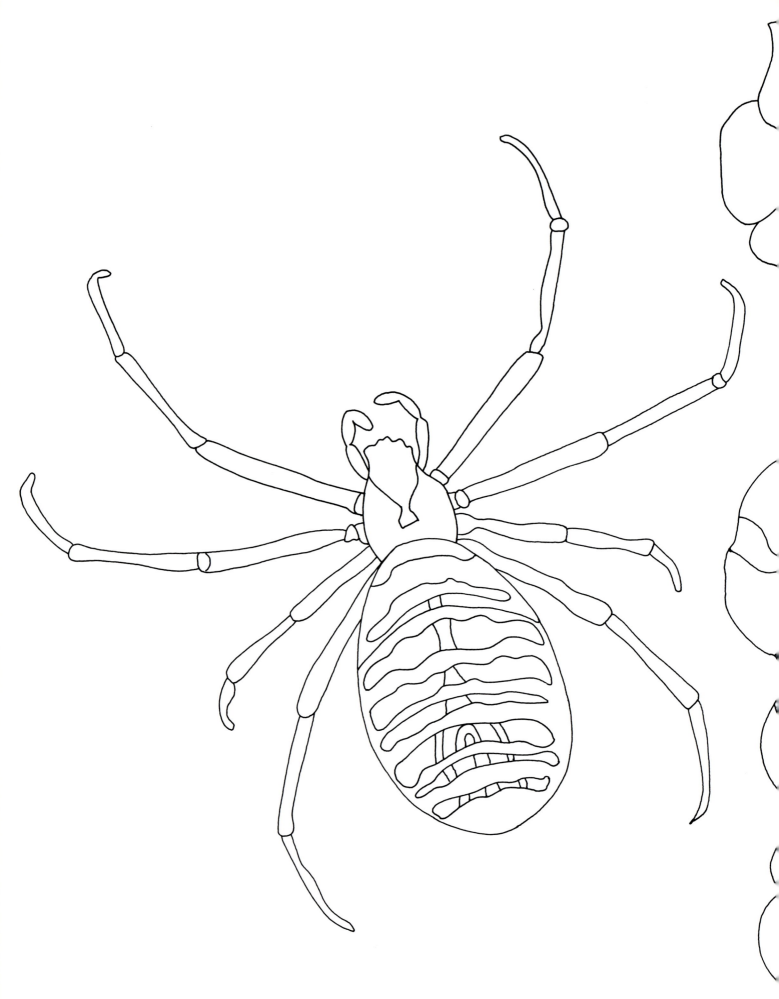

NASTURTIUMS

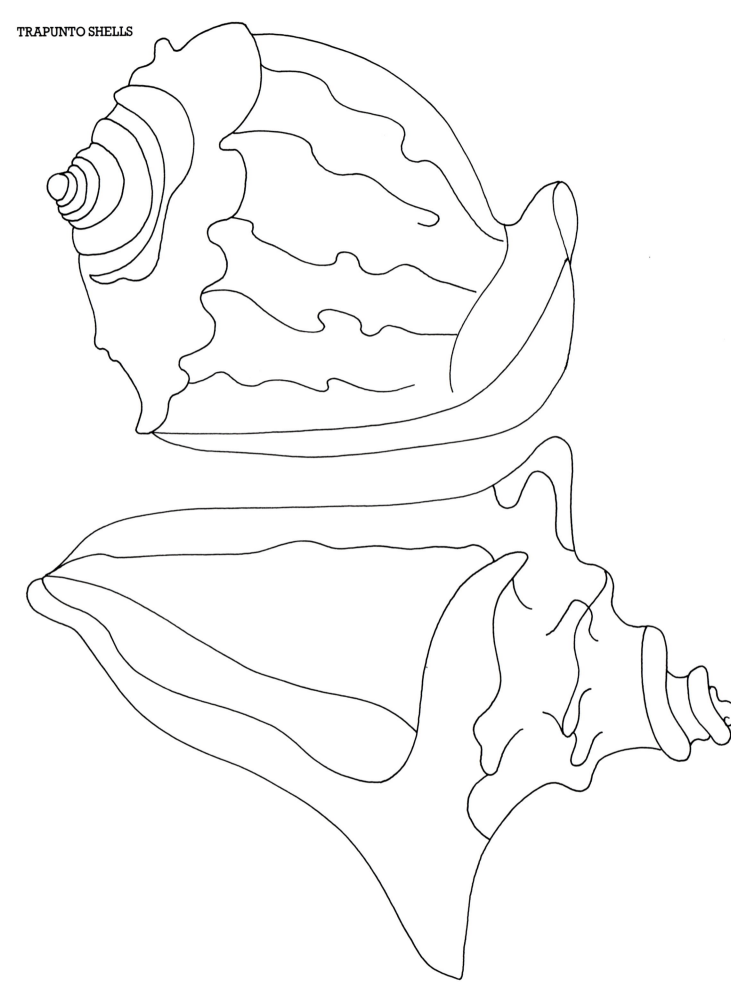

TRAPUNTO SHELLS

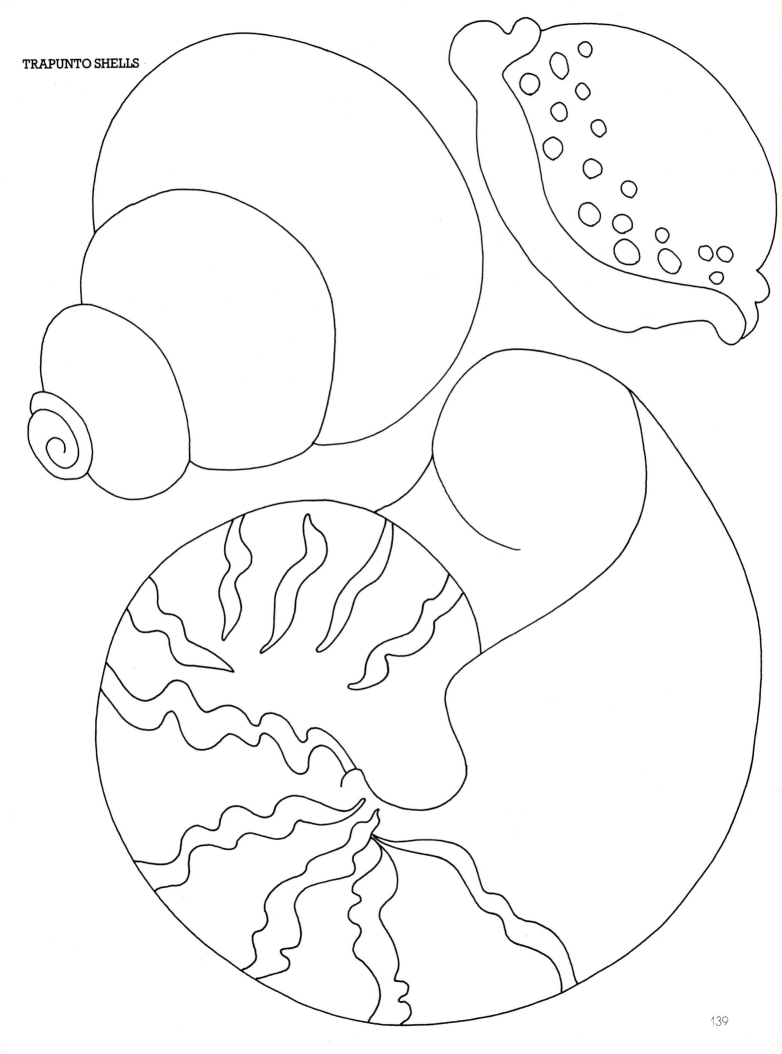

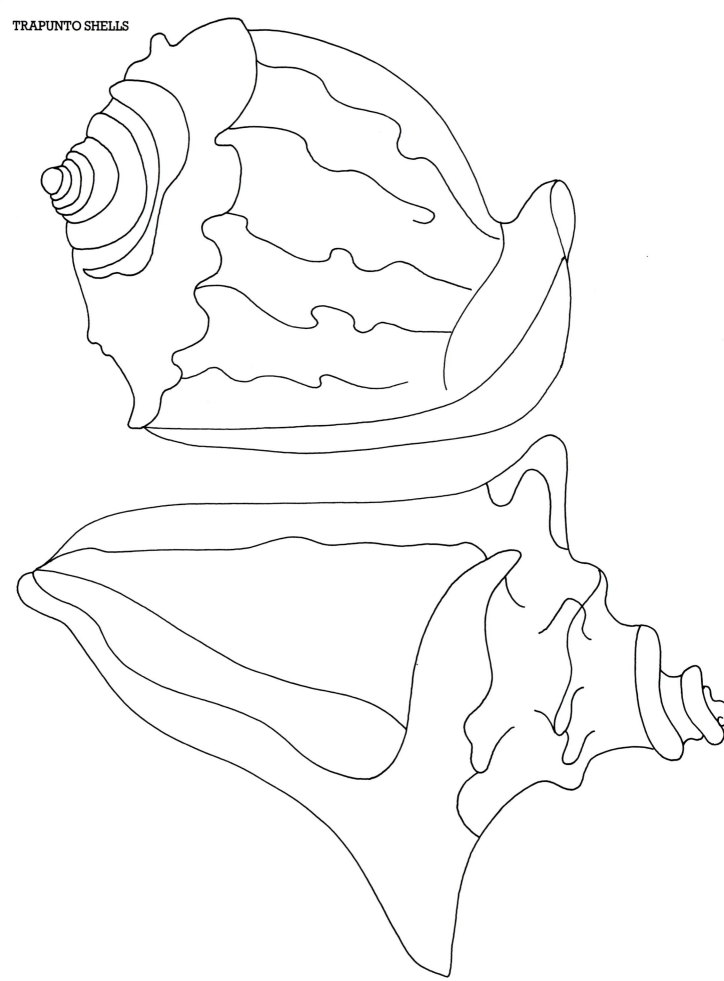

NASTURTIUMS

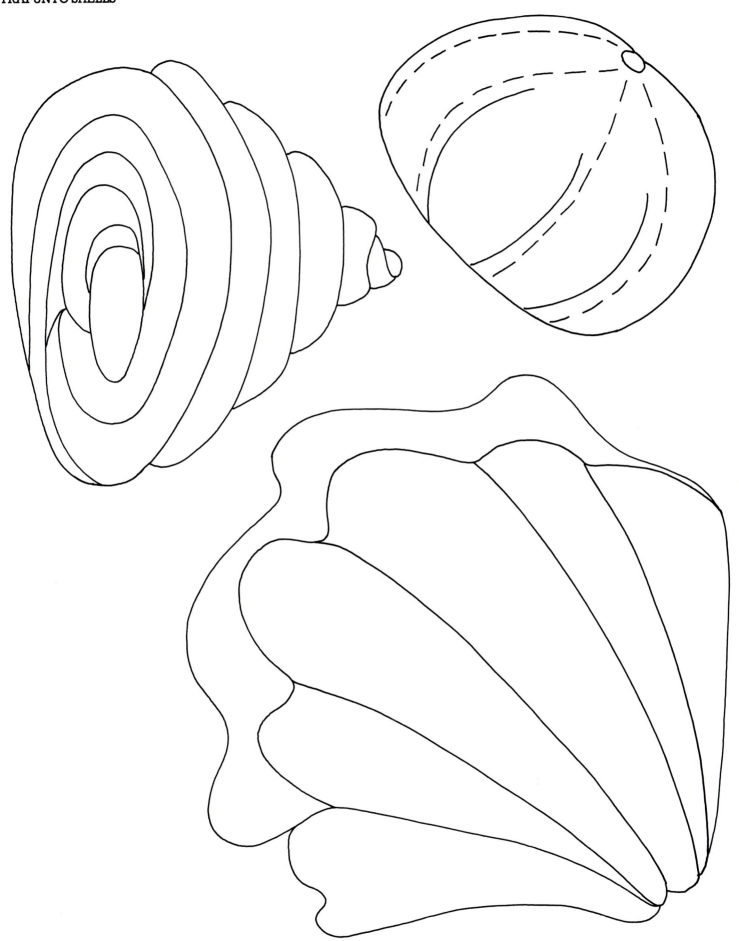

BLOSSOMS

COUNTRY KITCHEN (finished size 86 cm x 61 cm)

BISCUITS

PANDA

PANDA

WALL HANGING (finished size 86 cm x 61 cm)

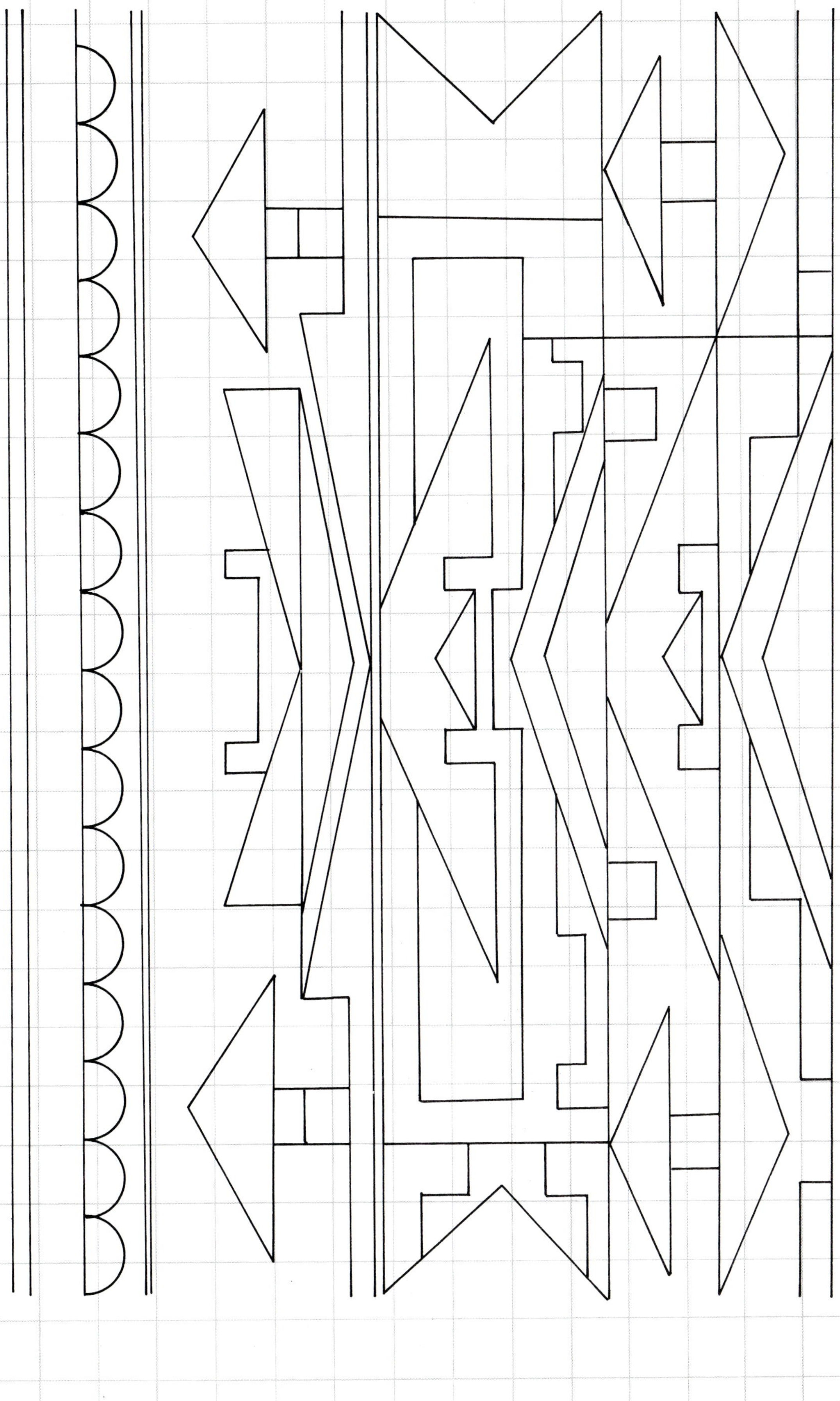

ENGLISH COUNTRY GARDEN (finished size 126 cm x 86 cm)

DOG ROSES (finished size of Wild Flowers 150 cm x 100 cm)

FRANGIPANI

FREESIAS

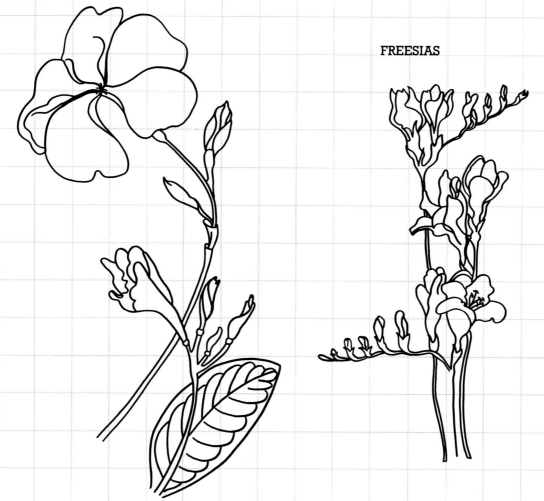

COSMOS

HERMES (enlarge to 45 cm)

MARATHON RUNNER

COSMOS (finished size 100 cm x 61 cm)

WHEAT FIELDS (finished size 86 cm x 61 cm)

TRAPUNTO ROSE

TROPICAL PARROT

SILK-MOTH (finished size 60 cm x 40 cm)

COCONUT PALMS

155

GIANT EGG (finished size 96 cm x 60 cm)

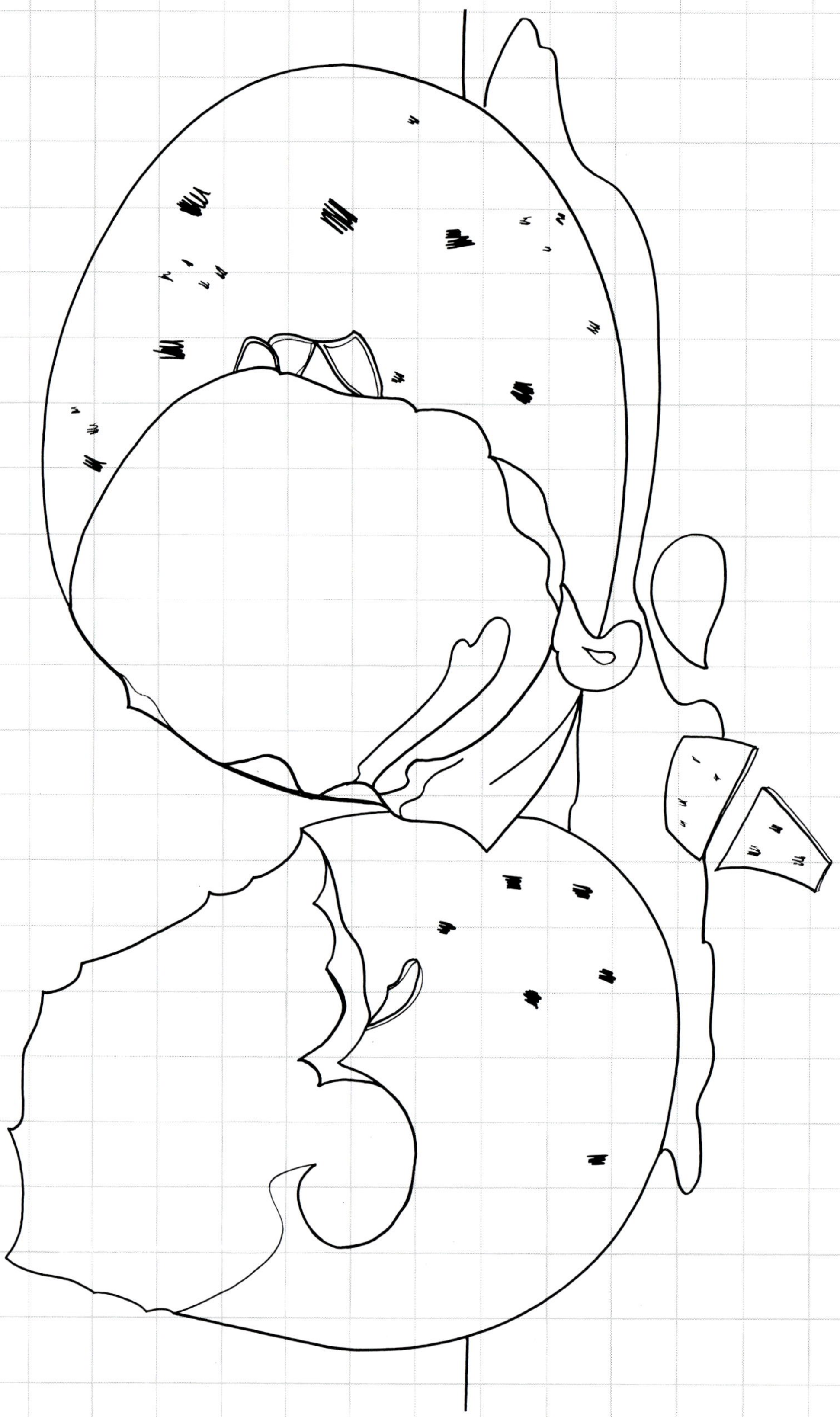

GLITTERING FROG

ARUM LILIES

WINDSURFING (finished size 100 cm x 80 cm)

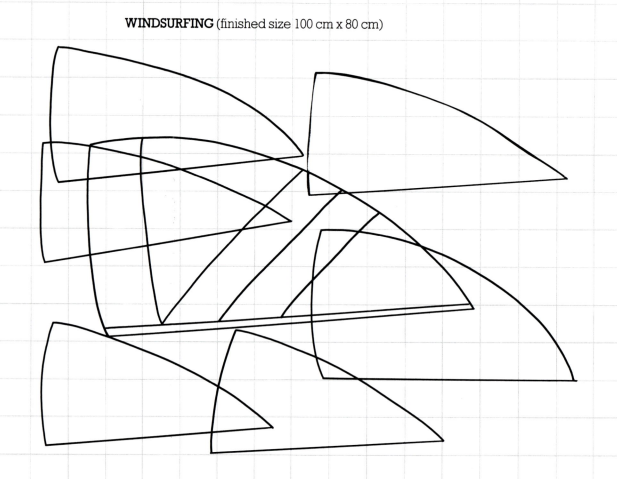

BEACH PALS (finished size 96 cm x 70 cm)

NDEBELE ARTIST (finished size 60 cm x 42 cm)

FIGHTING COCKS

IRISES

HERON

GOOSANDER WITH CHICKS

BIRD IN FLIGHT

161

TEA FOR TWO (finished size 102 cm x 96 cm)

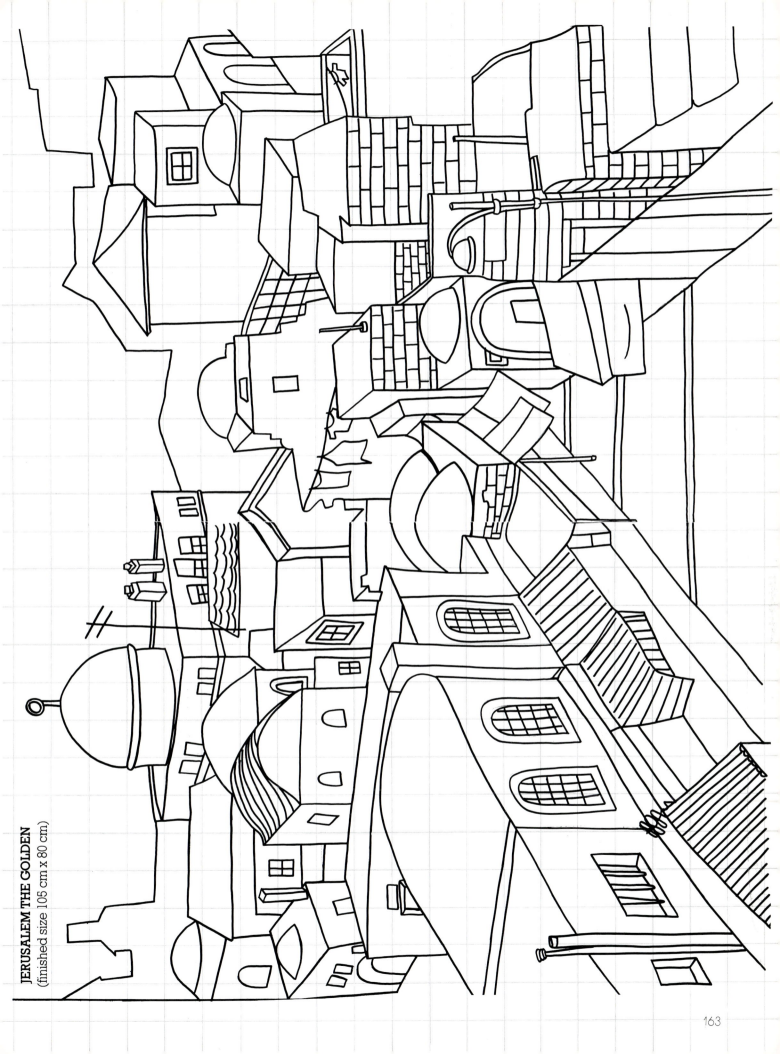

JERUSALEM THE GOLDEN
(finished size 105 cm x 80 cm)

163

ON SAFARI (finished size 135 cm x 95 cm)

EAGLE IN FLIGHT

LITTLE BLUE BIRD WITH CHICKS

DUCK

DRAKE

HARLEQUIN (finished size 80 cm x 70 cm)

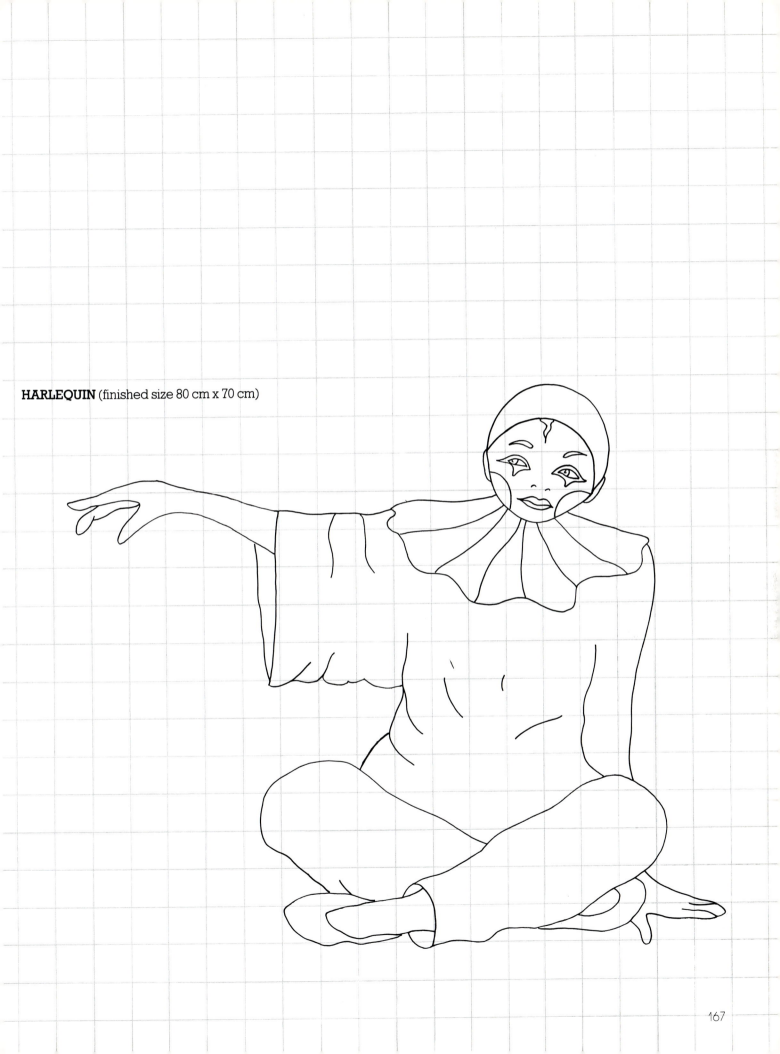

BRONZE EAGLE

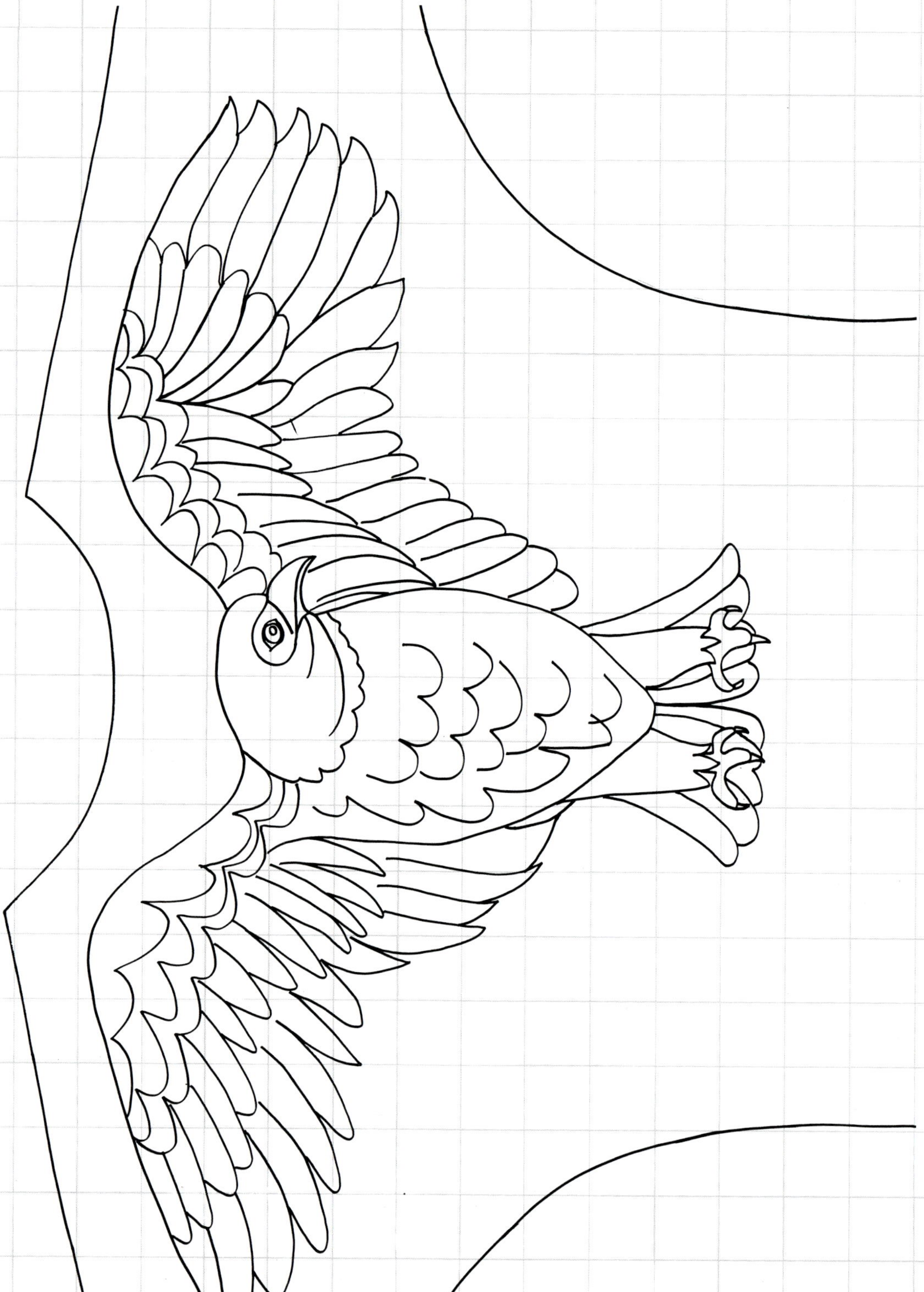

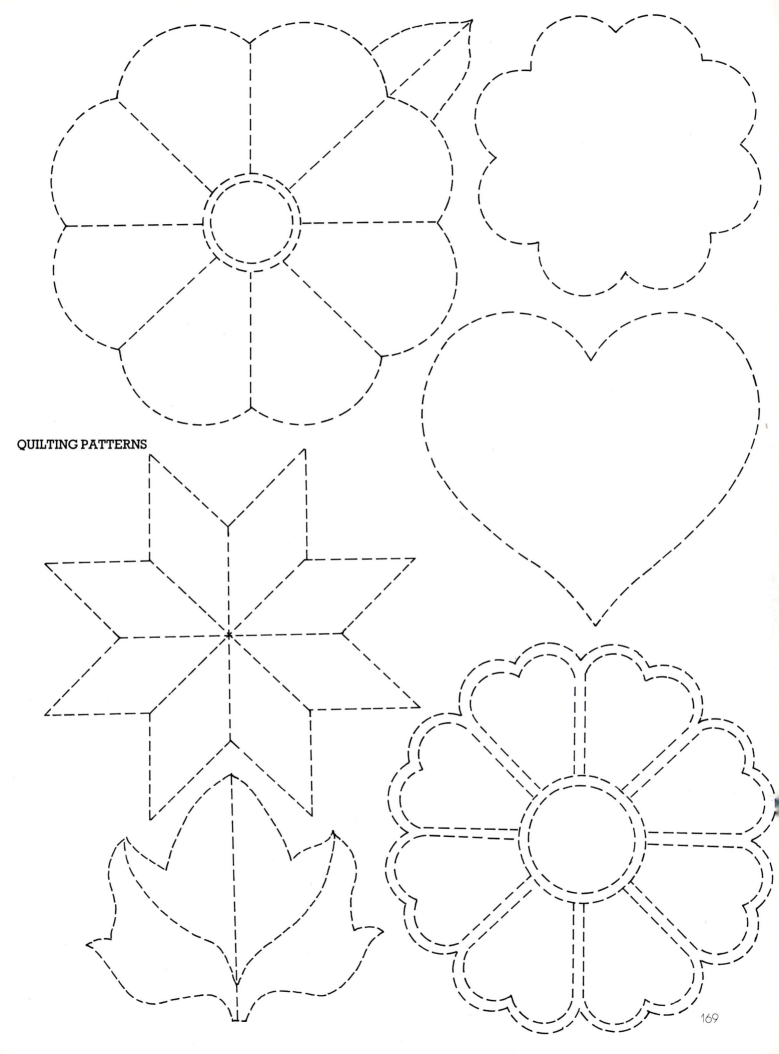

QUILTING PATTERNS

169

CIRCUS TRAIN (finished size 174 cm x 61 cm)

BIRD OF PARADISE

BELT

LITTLE DUCKS PRAM COVER (finished size 78 cm x 55 cm)

FOXGLOVES

GOLFING RAT (finished size 63,5 cm x 51 cm)

PETAL TEMPLATES

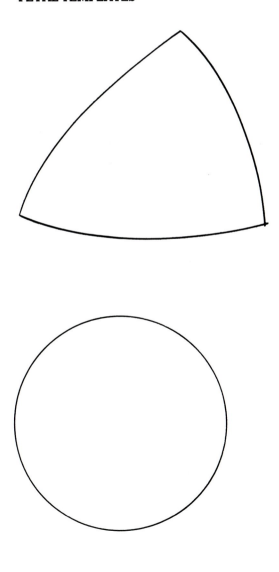

DRESS AND DUNGAREE PATTERNS seam allowances included

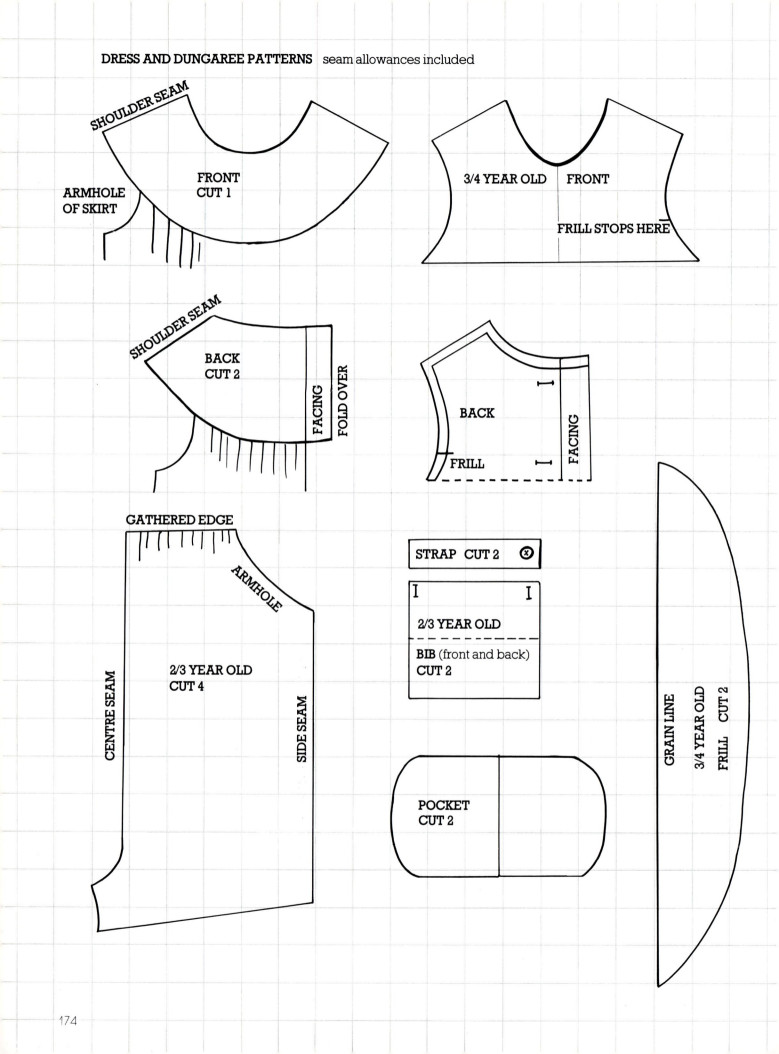

SHOULDER SEAM

FRONT
CUT 1

ARMHOLE
OF SKIRT

3/4 YEAR OLD   FRONT

FRILL STOPS HERE

SHOULDER SEAM

BACK
CUT 2

FACING

FOLD OVER

BACK

FRILL

FACING

GATHERED EDGE

ARMHOLE

CENTRE SEAM

2/3 YEAR OLD
CUT 4

SIDE SEAM

STRAP CUT 2 ⊗

2/3 YEAR OLD

BIB (front and back)
CUT 2

POCKET
CUT 2

GRAIN LINE

3/4 YEAR OLD

FRILL CUT 2

INDEX